Tips & Quips

for the Family Historian

Elizabeth Shown Mills
&
Ruth Brossette Lennon

2017
Genealogical Publishing Co.
Baltimore, Maryland

ISBN 978-0-8063-2041-0
Library of Congress CIP 2017932592

Designed & typeset by Ruth Brossette Lennon
Set in Constantia and Tempus Sans

Cover art:
Adapted from CanStockPhoto image csp9016561 by rup;
used under license

Page 3 quote:
Laurence Overmire, *Laurence Overmire*
(http://laurenceovermire.com/genealogy.html :
accessed 15 August 2016),
home page and "Quotes" tab.

History remembers only the celebrated.
Genealogy remembers them all.
　　　　　—Laurence Overmire

Categories

Accuracy 11
Analysis... 12
Ancestors & Ancestry.................................13
Brick Walls.. 16
Caution 18
Censuses 19
Certainty.. 20
Citations 21
Conclusions.. 22
Context 23
Creativity 24
Credentials 24
Discovery 25
Document Analysis....................................26
Documentation...27
Editing 28
Education 28
Elusive Ancestors 29
Errors 30
Ethics 31
Ethnic Research.. 32
Evidence 35
Facts.. 37
Families.. 38
Family Trees... 39
FAN Principle 40
Genealogical Proof Standard 41

Categories

Genealogy...43

Generalizations..48

Genetic Genealogy...................................49

Gullibilty..52

History..53

Hypotheses...55

Identity..56

Immigration...57

Information..58

Internet...59

Land..60

Learning..61

Lecturing...62

Luck..63

Maps & Mapping....................................64

Memoirs & Diaries.................................65

Methodology...66

Migration..67

Miscellany...68

Mistakes..70

Murphy's Law..71

Names...71

Negative Evidence.................................72

Negative Findings..................................73

Note Taking..73

Origins..74

Photographs...75

Plagiarism...76

Poor Folks...77

Privacy..78

Categories

Problem Solving...79
Professional Genealogy 81
Proof 84
Proof Statements 88
Quality.. 88
Questions 89
Reasonably Exhaustive Research 90
Records 92
Research 93
(The) Research Question 97
Research Traps 98
Roots... 99
Silence..100
Software..101
Solutions... 102
Sources.. 103
Standards... 105
Stories & Storytelling... 106
Success.. 108
Tax Records 109
Teaching 110
Traditions 111
Trivial Details 113
Trust...114
Truth 115
Uncertainty.. 117
Understanding 118
War..119
Writing 120

Appendixes

References 123
Index to Individuals Quoted 155
Index to Keywords 162

Tips &
Quips

Accuracy

Any one record can generate a million questions, but the most important question is this: How accurate is the information?[1]

—Dee Parmer Woodtor

A source's accuracy is unknown until the researcher has accumulated enough evidence for tests of correlation—the comparison and contrasting of sources and information to reveal points of agreement and disagreement.[2]

—Thomas W. Jones

It's not what we don't know
that hurts.
It's what we know that ain't so.[3]
—Will Rogers

There is too great a tendency among ancestor hunters to see how far back they can go rather than how accurate and complete they can be.[4]

—Val D. Greenwood

Analysis

Whether using a database or a document, the crucial question the researcher must ask is not "What does this say?" but "What does this mean?"[5]

—*GeLee Corley Hendrix*

You can have many documents or just a few documents but, without analysis, all you have is a bunch of documents.[6]

—*Debra Newman Carter*

Simple solutions seldom are. It takes a very unusual mind to undertake analysis of the obvious.[7]

—*Alfred North Whitehad*

Every [research] step involves two distinct activities: One is the search and the other is the analysis.[8]

—*Dee Parmer Woodtor*

The more important the subject and the closer it cuts to the bone of our hopes and needs, the more we are likely to err in establishing a framework for analysis.[9]

—*Stephen Jay Gould*

Ancestors & Ancestry

To forget one's ancestors is to be a brook
without a source, a tree without a root.
—Chinese Proverb

Knowledge of our ancestors shapes us and instills
within us values that give direction and meaning
to our lives.[10] —*Dennis B. Neuenschwander*

We stand tall today because we stand on the
shoulders of our ancestors.[11]
—*Roshni Mooneeram*

I am who I am, because of all the people
who have come before me.[12]
—*Louis Metoyer*

It is a desirable thing to be well-descended, but the
glory belongs to our ancestors.[13]
—*Plutarch*

We have no claim to share in the glory of our
ancestors unless we strive to resemble them.[14]
—*Jean Baptiste Poquelin alias Molière*

Ancestors & Ancestry

There are many kinds of conceit, but the chief
one is to let people know what a very ancient
and gifted family one descends from.[15]
—*Benvenuto Cellini*

He that has no fools, knaves, or beggars in
his family was begot by a flash of lightning.[16]
—*Thomas Fuller*

A man who prides himself on his ancestry
is like the potato plant, the best part of
which is under ground.
—Spanish Proverb

When our hearts turn to our ancestors, something
changes inside us. We feel part of something greater
than ourselves.[17]—*Russell M. Nelson*

A man can't very well make for himself a
place in the sun if he keeps continually
taking refuge under the family tree.[18]
—*Anonymous*

A man who boasts only of his ancestors confesses
that he belongs to a family that is better dead
than alive.[19]—*Abraham Lincoln (allegedly)*

∼Ancestors & Ancestry

[Heredity is] an omnibus in which all our ancestors
ride, and every now and then one of them
puts his head out and embarrasses us.[20]
—*Oliver Wendell Holmes I*

There is no king who has not had
a slave among his ancestors, and no slave
who has not had a king among his.[21]
—*Helen Keller*

**You should study the Peerage ...
It is the best thing in fiction
the English have ever done.[22]**
—*Oscar Wilde*

If you are ashamed to have ancestors who do
not meet your own social standards,
then stay away from your genealogy.[23]
—*Val D. Greenwood*

**Let's face it.
We're all wimps compared to our ancestors.[24]**
—*Megan Smolenyak Smolenyak*

All have made me who I am. I stand on their
shoulders and I am forever indebted to their hard
work and sacrifice.[25]
—*Tony Burroughs*

Brick Walls

A brick wall in genealogy is not a dead end.
It's an invitation to build a ladder.[26]
—*Elizabeth Shown Mills*

All of your genealogical brick walls can be scaled or knocked down. Yes, all of them. ... There may be walls we cannot break down in our lifetime, but with good thorough research and perseverance, we should be able to lay the groundwork and weaken that wall for genealogists in the future.[27]
—*Michael D. Lacopo*

People who avoid the brick walls—all power to ya. But we all have to hit them sometimes in order to push through to the next level, to evolve.[28]

—*Jennifer Aniston*

**What the caterpillar calls the end of the world,
the master calls a butterfly.[29]
—*Richard Bach***

Novice genealogists create their own "brick walls" by not locating all the records that may be relevant to the research question and ultimately missing those needed to solve the problem.[30]

—*Angela Packer McGhie*

So many times, as researchers, we handicap ourselves. We are in such a hurry to eliminate possibilities that we eliminate possibilities.[31]

—Elizabeth Shown Mills

True genealogists refuse to
live in houses with brick walls.

—*Anonymous*

**I attribute my success to this:
I never gave or took any excuse.[32]
—*Florence Nightingale***

Brick walls—
that overused euphemism for
poor research methods.[33]

—*Edgar E. McDonald*

Caution

Don't fall in love with the first record you see.
Or any of them, really.[34]
—*Harold Henderson*

The past is a foreign
country: they do things
differently there.[35]
—L. P. Hartley

Inexperienced researchers often stumble when
they rely too much on what feels familiar and fall
back on kinds of argument they already know. ...
If as a psychology or biology major you learned to
gather hard data and subject them to statistical
analysis, do not assume that you can do the same
in ... history.[36]

—*Wayne C. Booth et al.*

Censuses

A census is a snapshot taken at one isolated moment in a person's life. It freezes that person in a household or a situation—but that situation may have not been true for him the day before the census or the day after.[37]
—*Elizabeth Shown Mills*

Think of the census as what the census taker recorded—not necessarily what the truth is.[38]
—*Dee Parmer Woodtor*

Certainty

A huge percentage

of the stuff that I tend

to be automatically

certain of is, it turns

out, totally wrong and

deluded.[39]

—David Foster Wallace

Citations

Citations help you establish the credibility of your conclusion from the evidence you find.[40]
—*Thomas W. Jones*

Constructing citations is [mostly] about following patterns. Published materials typically follow one pattern; unpublished sources follow another. Website citations are similar in pattern to those for print publications. Different patterns distinguish reference notes (footnotes and endnotes) and bibliographic entries. Researchers familiar with the basic patterns will be able to comfortably cite many sources.[41]
—*Alison Hare*

Our citations tell readers exactly what we used and whether or not our conclusions and claims of proof rest on likely accurate sources.[42]
—*Thomas W. Jones*

Conclusions

**Genealogical evidence is a possibility,
not a conclusion.**[43]
—*Thomas W. Jones*

No historical conclusion amounts to "Case Closed."
Unknown evidence might still emerge
to change a conclusion.[44]
—Elizabeth Shown Mills

If you reach a different conclusion than another researcher,
don't just stubbornly say, "I'm right and you're wrong."
Prove it. Either try to work backwards from their evidence
to see if you can reach their conclusion or ask them for
the evidence that led them to that conclusion and follow
it. It will either prove enlightening for you or enable you
to show them where they went wrong.[45]   *—Carol Baxter*

Proof is a fundamental concept in genealogy.
In order to merit confidence, each conclusion
about an ancestor must have sufficient credibility
to be accepted as "proved." Acceptable conclusions,
therefore, meet the Genealogical Proof Standard.[46]
—Elissa Scalise Powell

**When we explain our reasoning and show
our documentation, others can see that our
conclusions are reliable.**[47] **—*Thomas W. Jones***

Context

Births, marriages, and deaths are the bare bones of family history. Historical context is the setting against which those events occurred. Recreating that setting [is] a task of vital importance if we want to understand what shaped an ancestor's life.[48]

—Alison Hare

Do not consider the research complete if the person being pursued is not yet placed in the context of family, community, and time.[49]
—David McDonald

Failure to understand the context of a document can lead to false assumptions.[50]
—Barbara Vines Little

Creativity

We cannot create records,
but success comes to those
who use records creatively.[51]
—*Elizabeth Shown Mills*

||||||||||||||||||||||||||||||||||||||||||||||||||||||||||||||||||||||||||||||||||||||||||

Credentials

Certification helped develop my abilities
in genealogical problem solving and
presenting complex evidence. Accreditation
improved how I approach timed research
and reporting. Clients generally recognize
the value of credentials, even when they are
not familiar with the exact process.[52]
—*Paul K. Graham*

Discovery

The joy of discovery is
certainly the liveliest
that the mind of man
can ever feel.[53]
—Claude Bernard

Document Analysis

> "Everything we see hides another thing; we always want to see what is hidden by what we see.[54]
>
> —René Magritte

Documentation

Genealogy without documentation
is mythology.
—*Anonymous*

**Too much documentation
always trumps too little.**[55]
—*Thomas W. Jones*

In God we trust.
All others must show sources.[56]
—*David Woody*

Editing

A good writer is not necessarily a
good editor, and vice versa.[57]
—*Pamela K. Sayer*

Even editors need an editor when
they do their own writing.[58]
—*Elizabeth Shown Mills*

Education

We don't know what
we don't know.[59]
—*Elissa Scalise Powell*

Elusive Ancestors

> *To find parents or origin we focus our search upon the earliest proved place of residence. Our best clues to who he is and where he came from will be right there— even if that place is a "burned" county.[60]*
> *—Elizabeth Shown Mills*

Errors

Because published errors are
immortal, an error of omission
is always preferable to an error
of commission.[61]
—Robert Charles Anderson

Don't demand greater accuracy from records
than you are capable of yourself.[62]
—*Michael John Neill*

Be pleased, not peeved,
when someone wants to
verify your research.[63]
—Roger D. Joslyn

Ethics

Ethnic Research

First work methodically through records basic to research. Then zero in on sources unique to your ancestor's ethnic group, nationality, religion, geographic area, or time period.[65]

—*Paula Stuart-Warren*

(African Americans)

Genealogy enables African Americans to have a legacy of our ancestors' struggles, successes, and failures so that we can learn from our ancestor's lives—not to repeat their mistakes but to emulate their successes and use them as inspiration for the future.[66] —*Tony Burroughs*

The genealogical pursuit is therefore all about reclaiming the past and rewriting the experiences of our ancestors, both free and enslaved. For African Americans ... it is all about rebuilding a lost collective memory.[67]

—*Dee Parmer Woodtor*

Researching your ancestors during slavery becomes researching the owners of your ancestors.[68]
—*Nancy Richey*

A genealogist must be thorough. The more thorough you are between now and the slavery period, the more successful your research will be.[69]
—***Tony Burroughs***

Troubled silence is a part of the African American collective memory: silence about specific events, silence about ancestry, ... and even selective "dis-remembering" of ancestry.[70]
—*Dee Parmer Woodtor*

(Creoles)

Creole is a culture, not a color.[71]
—Terrel A. Delphin et al.

Ethnic Research

(Jewish Americans)

There are four great myths about tracing Jewish ancestry:
1. Nobody remembers them.
2. All the records were destroyed in the Holocaust.
3. Our family name was changed at Ellis Island.
4. We can't determine the town we came from in the Old Country.[72]

—Gary Mokotoff

(Native Americans)

The first and best rule is this: Proceed to research the family as if the Indian tradition did not exist. As the ancestral lines of the presumed Indian are extended back, a Native American connection (or clues to one) could surface in any type of record.[73]
—Rachal Mills Lennon

Researching Indian ancestors
does not mean researching
just Indian records.[74]
—Paula Stuart-Warren

Evidence

Evidence is evidence, whether words, numbers,
images, diagrams, still or moving.[75]
—Edward Tufte

**Without a research question,
genealogical evidence does not exist.[76]
*—Thomas W. Jones***

A lot of evidence lies in the spaces between records.
Using tax lists as an example, one can witness the
descendancy of land through the generations by
noting the acreage taxed [to] people over a long period
of time. This evidence is certainly based on a series of
records, but the whole is far greater than the sum of the
facts.[77]   *—Michael G. Hait*

Evidence can be messy.
Because it is a mental construct,
it rarely gives us the clear and
simple answers that we seek.[78]
—Elizabeth Shown Mills

**Genealogical evidence is a possibility,
not a conclusion.[79]   *—Thomas W. Jones***

Some circumstantial evidence is very strong,
as when you find a trout in the milk.[80]
—Henry David Thoreau

Evidence

All genealogists must have the ability to examine two records and determine if there is enough evidence to conclude that both belong to the same person.[81]

—*Robert Raymond*

(Conflicting Evidence)

"Contradictory evidence seldom puzzles the man who has mastered the laws of evidence, but he knows little of the laws of evidence who has not studied the unwritten law of the human heart.[82]

—*Edward George Earle Bulwer-Lytton*

**You live out the confusions
until they become clear.[83]**

—*Anaïs Nin*

If the results of a DNA test conflict with documentary evidence, then these conflicts must be resolved in order to satisfy the GPS [Genealogical Proof Standard].[84]

—*Blaine T. Bettinger*

Ignoring any conflicting evidence
could raise avoidable questions about
your research, reasoning, and results.[85]

—*Thomas W. Jones*

Facts

Facts get recorded.
Stories get remembered.[86]
—*Lewis Schiff*

**Fact explains nothing.
On the contrary,
it is fact that requires
explanation.[87]
—*Marilynne Robinson*

Doing genealogy is not a cold gathering
of facts but, instead, breathing life into all
who have gone before.[88]
—*Della M. Cummings Wright*

Families

Accidents will occur in the best
regulated families.[89]
—*Charles Dickens*

Family faces are magic mirrors.
Looking at people who belong to us,
we see the past, present, and future.[90]
—*Gail Lumet Buckley*

**If you think your family is normal,
you probably aren't a genealogist.**

—*Anonymous*

Can a first cousin, once removed, be returned?
—*Anonymous*

Call it a clan, call it a network,
call it a tribe, call it a family.
Whatever you call it,
whoever you are,
you need one.[91]
—*Jane Howard*

Other things may change us,
but we start and end with family.[92]
—*Anthony Brandt*

Family Trees

Some family trees have beautiful leaves and some have just a bunch of nuts. It is the nuts that make the tree worth shaking. —*Anonymous*

Before you link, think![93]
—*Elizabeth Shown Mills*

A couple of hours on the Internet,
a trip to the library, and we can fill
in the whole family tree.[94]
—"Frasier Crane"

Are the names adorning your family tree
really your ancestors—or just
crowd-sourced fiction?[95]
—*Megan Smolenyak Smolenyak*

FAN Principle

To prove identity, origin, and parentage,
study individuals in the context of their FAN Club:
Friends & Family, Associates, and Neighbors.[96]
—*Elizabeth Shown Mills*

**In a society where kinships were extensive
and daily life challenging, associations
were rarely random. They may be the only
way to prove relationships.[97]
—*Rachal Mills Lennon***

Our ancestors did not live in a vacuum. Like us, they too were surrounded by family members, associates, and neighbors. They interacted with these people, sometimes on a daily basis and sometimes only on occasion. The members of their FAN Club often hold the answers to their identity.[98]

—*Kay Haviland Freilich*

Genealogical Proof Standard

The Genealogical Proof Standard (GPS) is the standard for judging whether a statement made about a relationship, identity, situation, or event is substantially credible.[99] —*Thomas W. Jones*

The GPS might be described as a ruler.
It does not tell genealogical carpenters
how to cut through a board.
It tells them whether or not
they cut it too short.[100]
—Harold Henderson

Proof is a fundamental concept in genealogy. In order to merit confidence, each conclusion about an ancestor must have sufficient credibility to be accepted as "proved." Acceptable conclusions, therefore, meet the Genealogical Proof Standard.[101]
—*Elissa Scalise Powell*

Genealogical Proof Standard

The GPS is a standard of credibility.
It describes the level careful family historians
accept as adequate for proving relationships,
events, or any aspect of identity.[102]
—*Thomas W. Jones*

If a single aspect of the proof standard remains unmet, our conclusion cannot be considered sufficiently proved. The professional should honestly communicate this to clients, both before and after the research has been conducted.[103] —*Michael G. Hait*

**If the results of a DNA test conflict with
documentary evidence, then these
conflicts must be resolved
in order to satisfy the GPS.[104]
—*Blaine T. Bettinger***

Genealogy programs allow users to record numerous facts. However, the Genealogical Proof Standard requires genealogists to conduct thorough research for all relevant information and knowledgeably analyze all evidence before reaching a conclusion [about any fact]. Until research has met all of the proof standard's conditions, a genealogist cannot consider any conclusion proved.[105] —*Michael G. Hait*

Genealogy

Genealogy:
Tracing yourself back to people better than you.[106]
—*John Garland Pollard*

Genealogy is the study of families in genetic and historical
context. It is the study of communities, in which kinship
networks weave the fabric of economic, political, and
social life. It is the study of family situations and the
changing roles of men, women, and children in diverse
cultures. It is biography, reconstructing each human life
across place and time.[107]
—*Board for Certification of Genealogists*

By searching for our roots,
we come closer together as a human family.[108]
—*Orrin Hatch*

**Family history lets me give voice to long
forgotten souls who were dehumanized
by the bonds of slavery.[109]   —*Ruth Randall***

A life that is not documented is a life that
within a generation or two will largely be lost
to memory.[110]
—Dennis B. Neuenschwander

Genealogy

We all feel stronger if we are part of a tapestry. One thread alone is weak, but, woven into something larger, surrounded by other threads, it is more difficult to unravel.[111]

—*Stefan Walters*

The more you know of your history,
the more liberated you become.[112]
—Maya Angelou

**The greatest gifts you can give your children are
the roots of responsibility and
the wings of independence.[113]
—*Dennis Waitley***

Genealogy—
Chasing your own tale.
—Anonymous

"Taking someone the past has forgotten,
discovering their identity, recreating their
existence, and etching their life story into
the annals of history has to be the most
rewarding challenge one could have as a
historian or genealogist.[114]
—*Elizabeth Shown Mills*

The more you investigate the lives of
seemingly ordinary people, the more
remarkable they become.[115]
—*Anthony Powell*

Genealogy is not fatal—but it's a grave disease.
—*Anonymous*

The central organizing principle in the discipline
of genealogy is the analysis of kinship.[116]
—*Carolyn Earle Billingsley*

Genealogy

Genealogy isn't about being a collector of names and dates. It's about being a collector of stories and struggles, successes and failures. It's about finding and documenting the truth, whatever that truth may be, regardless of how uncomfortable it might be to acknowledge it.[117]

—*Chris Staats*

None of us can harbor prejudice against another group of people when we realize that, with the very next document we find, we could be a part of them.[118]
—Elizabeth Shown Mills

We are the chosen ones. In each family there is one who seems called to find the ancestors. To put flesh on their bones and make them live again. To tell of their family story and to feel that somehow they know and approve. Doing genealogy is not a cold gathering of facts but, instead, breathing life into all who have gone before. We are the story tellers of the tribe. All tribes have one. We have been called by those who have gone before.[119]

—*Della M. Cummings Wright*

**We don't own our family history.
We simply preserve it for the next generation."[120]
—*Rosemary Alva*

Beneath the fun of stalking one's ancestors and relatives is the humbling realization that each of us is merely a link in a chain. We may someday be forgotten, but the contribution we made to the chain will always be there, and as long as the chain exists, a piece of us will exist, too.[121] —*Dan Rottenberg*

Genealogy can not only help kids understand the world but can give them respect for their elders, bridge generation gaps, and heal family wounds.[122]
—*Tony Burroughs*

Knowledge of our ancestors shapes us and instills within us values that give direction and meaning to our lives.[123]
—*Dennis B. Neuenschwander*

The heart and soul of genealogy is uncovering and learning the stories of our ancestors. It's all about them, not us. If your end goal is name collecting or name dropping, you're making it about you. It's the historical version of a selfie.[124]
—*Megan Smolenyak Smolenyak*

When a society or a civilization perishes, one condition can always be found. They forgot where they came from.[125] —*Carl Sandburg*

Generalizations

All
generalizations
are false,
including this one.[126]
— Mark Twain

Genetic Genealogy

People lie. DNA doesn't.[127]
—Angie Bush

DNA information can statistically support a genealogical paper trail. It does not replace it. It does not prove exact relationships once we move past our parents and siblings.[128]
—Debbie Parker Wayne

People seem to believe that unless genetic and social genealogy match up, genealogy is irrelevant to them.[129]
—Eva Goodwin

DNA evidence is among the types of evidence a knowledgeable researcher would seek, and so it is within the scope of the reasonably exhaustive search, if suitable donors can be identified and consent to testing. If none can be found, the "reasonably exhaustive search" requirement has been satisfied, and the paper evidence can stand on its own.[130]
—Donn Devine

Genetic Genealogy

A genetic genealogist must consider the emotional implications of DNA findings. When DNA tests provide information a family may not want to believe, the genealogist must lay a foundation to encourage its acceptance.[131] —*Debbie Parker Wayne*

If the results of a DNA test conflict with documentary evidence, then these conflicts must be resolved in order to satisfy the Genealogical Proof Standard.[132]
—*Blaine T. Bettinger*

No area of family history poses more ethical questions than genetic genealogy— dealing with the secrets locked away in our genes.[133]—*Judy G. Russell*

Knowing your haplogroup can act as a GPS — a genealogical positioning system to help you better understand where your line originated.[134]
—*Diahan Southard*

The absence of matching DNA doesn't always mean the lack of a common ancestor.[135]
—Debbie Parker Wayne

Genetic Genealogy

For people from nontraditional families, genetics are not the whole picture. Bloodlines alone will not give them answers to questions about memories, stories, traditions, values, spiritual beliefs, and forms of care. These things are inherited through human contact over time, not through biology or genetics.[136]

—*Eva Goodwin*

A living [male] tested today can almost exactly represent every ancestor on a direct paternal line for at least 8 generations and up to 12 or more. This means that you have an original document from 8 generations ago right inside of you.[137]

—***Diahan Southard***

Successful use of DNA tests requires understanding how to interpret the tests and how to use the tools.[138]

—Elizabeth Shown Mills

Genetic genealogy is not used in a vacuum. It is only useful when comparing results from two or more people.[139]

—*Debbie Parker Wayne*

Gullibility

It must be true.

I seen it in print.

(Favorite Proverb of Morons)[140]

—Donald Lines Jacobus

History

—

Every day of your life
is a page of
your history.
—*Anonymous*

—

History —

Most everything we think of as natural is historical and has roots—specifically in the late eighteenth and early nineteenth centuries, the so-called Romantic revolutionary period—and we're essentially still dealing with expectations and feelings that were formulated at that time.[141] —*Susan Sontag*

It is not deeds or acts that last:
it is the written record of those
deeds and acts.[142]
—Elbert Hubbard

History is always an invention; it is a fairy tale built upon certain clues. The clues are not the problem. These clues are pretty well established; most of them can literally be laid on the desktop for anyone to handle. But these ... do not constitute history. History consists of the links between them, and it is this that presents the problem.[143] —*Peter Hoeg*

**A people without the knowledge of
their past history, origin and culture
is like a tree without roots.[144]
—Marcus Garvey**

Hypotheses

There are two possible outcomes:
If the result confirms the hypothesis,
then you've made a discovery.
If the result is contrary to the hypothesis,
then you've made a discovery.[145]
—*Enrico Fermi*

//

**Don't believe
everything you think.**[146]
—*Thomas E. Kida*

Identity

You must have a sound, explicit reason
for saying that any two individual records
refer to the same person.[147]
—*Robert Charles Anderson*

> Identity is more than a name.
> It is every known detail of a human life.[148]
> —*Elizabeth Shown Mills*

All genealogists must have the ability to examine two
records and determine if there is enough evidence to
conclude that both belong to the same person.[149]
—*Robert Raymond*

To prove identity, origin, and parentage,
study individuals in the context of their
FAN Club:
Friends & Family,
Associates, and Neighbors.[150]
—Elizabeth Shown Mills

Immigration

> People did not always
> emigrate to the area of their
> first choice.
> It depended on which
> colony or ... country
> were running schemes at
> the time when people were
> considering leaving.[151]
>
> —Helen V. Smith

Information

Just because a piece of
information exists does
not mean it can be accepted
as fact. Behind each shred
of data lies an informant,
the person who provided it.
Genealogists must consider
both the information
and its origin—the
informant—to appraise the
information's accuracy.[152]
—*Laura Murphy DeGrazia*

Information helps us solve a specific
problem. Knowledge helps us solve many
problems.[153]
—*Elizabeth Shown Mills*

Internet

To simply type a name of someone into Google
or such is sorta like aiming your shotgun from
the back door toward the woods,
hoping to kill game for supper.[154]
—*Paul Drake*

You won't find everything sitting
on your butt all day in front of
your computer.[155]
—*Fern K. Buford-Walker*

Surfing's fun. But surf contains a lot of
froth and some scum.[156]
—Penelope Christensen

Too many fishers of the 'Net become
fish because they take the bait.
Don't let that be you.[157]
—*Terrence M. Punch*

**If you look long enough,
you can find someone who will back up most
anything you want to say.[158]
—*Paul Rawlings***

Land

The descent of land
is the purest proof of kinship.[159]
—*Richard S. Lackey*

A lot of evidence lies in the
spaces between records. Using
tax lists as an example, one
can witness the descendancy
of land through the generations by noting the acreage
taxed [to] people over a long
period of time. This evidence
is certainly based on a series
of records, but the whole is
far greater than the sum of the
facts.[160]

*Michael
Hait*

Learning

The ancestors who give us the
most trouble are usually the ones
who teach us the most.[161]
—*Stefani Evans*

Wherever you are in family history,
you're always in learning mode.[162]
—Don Anderson

I thought I was an advanced genealogist.
Then I downgraded to advanced
beginner. Now I am thinking: Let's just
start over and say I'm a beginner with
some background in the subject.[163]
—*Jacqueline Wilson*

**It's what we learn
after we think we know it all
that counts.[164]
—*Kim Hubbard***

Lecturing

What the audience needs
is more important than what you want to say.[165]
—*Paul Milner*

||||||||||||||||||||||||||||||||||||||||||||||||||||||||||||||||||||

You have to talk to each specific
audience. All of your lecture
preparation can fall flat if you don't
focus on who your audience will be
and ways to successfully engage and
maintain their interest.[166]
—George G. Morgan

Luck

Luck happens when
the well-prepared
mind meets
opportunity.[167]
—*Elissa Scalise Powell*

⁓

Remember that not getting what you want
is sometimes a wonderful stroke of luck.[168]
—*Tenzin Gyatso, 14th Dalai Lama*

Maps & Mapping

Combining maps with other documents,
especially land records and censuses,
can bring out details that
no one document contains.[169]
—*Daniel Hubbard*

**Jurisdictional lines are far more significant to
us, when using a map, than they were to our
ancestors who simply looked down a road.[170]
—*Michael G. Hait***

Mapping the rooms of a favorite house,
the occupants of neighboring houses,
or a daily journey to work or school can
revive memories of a place and the events
and people associated with that place.[171]
—*Stefani Evans*

Memoirs & Diaries

**When it comes to our personal histories,
we're all revisionists, struggling, usually
unconsciously, to place our past in the best
light, to see ourselves as virtuous.[172]
—James Dannenberg**

||||||||||||||||||||||||||||||||||||||||||||||||||||||||||||||||||||||

My truth as I remember it
becomes fact because of my fame.
I write what I feel.
It is not a historical account.
No memory ever is. I exaggerate.
I, like Armistead Maupin,
jewel the elephant.[173]
—Rosie O'Donnell

Methodology

The manner in which we research
—the methodology—
can often determine what we are able to find,
especially when clues are scarce.[174]
—*Ruth Ann Abels Hager*

Genealogical method is similar to scientific method. After some preliminary research, we make a hypothesis. ... If we find conflicting evidence that cannot be resolved, we may need to modify our hypothesis and then do more research. If, after a good deal of research, the hypothesis is still standing, we draw a cautious conclusion.[175] —*J. H. "Jay" Fonkert*

Migration

When I get ready to move,
I just shut the door,
call the hogs, and git!
—*American Folk Saying*

Over the decades, perhaps the wrong questions have been asked about the Great Migration. Perhaps it is not a question of whether the migrants brought good or ill to the cities they fled to or were pushed or pulled to their destinations, but a question of how they summoned the courage to leave in the first place.[176]

—*Isabel Wilkerson*

When the bark pops off the fence
rails, it's time to move on.
—American Folk Saying

Miscellany

Your life is made of two dates and a dash.
Make the most of the dash.
—*Anonymous*

**A stumbing block is often
a stepping stone.**
—**Anonymous**

There is no Genealogists Anonymous
because no one wants to quit.
—*Anonymous*

**Genealogy is not a race to the finish
but a journey through time.**
—*Anonymous*

It is as though our ancestors want to be found.
Uncanny coincidences. Olympian luck. Phenomenal
fate. Tremendous intuition. Remarkable miracles.
We call it "Serendipity in Genealogy.[177]
—*Robert Raymond*

There are no premature babies—
just delayed weddings.
—*American Folk Saying*

One of the worst things a
genealogist can do is to get
to the destination before
making the journey.[178]
—*Henry Z Jones Jr*

In Boston they ask,
"How much does he know?"
In New York, "How much is
he worth." In Philadelphia,
"Who were his parents."[179]
—*Mark Twain*

**The family historian wants to remember
what their grandparents wished to forget.[180]
—*Diedre Erin Denton***

Mistakes

Don't cling to a mistake
just because you
spent a lot of time making it.[181]
—*Randy Cantrell*

—⁓—

He who says
he never made a mistake
is either a liar or a fool.[182]
—*Donald Lines Jacobus*

Murphy's Law

Murphy's law as applied to genealogy:
There is a negative correlation between the
importance of a record and its legibility.[183]

—*Yvette Hoitink*

|||||||||||||||||||||||||||||||||||||||||||||||||||||||||||||||||||||||||||||||||||||||

Names

"Name's the same"
doesn't mean the person is.[184]
—*Elizabeth Shown Mills*

Negative
Evidence

The historian must respect
contextually suggestive silence.
It must be plumbed, found to be
true—or not —and brought into
arguments where it is relevant.[185]
—David Henige

||||||||||||||||||||||||||||||||||||||||||||||||||||||||||||||||||||||||||||

Negative evidence:
Conclusions or implications that can be drawn
from the absence of a situation or information
that should exist given the circumstances.

Caution:
Negative evidence is not the same as negative
findings. Merely not finding what we hope to
find is a routine matter in historical research
and one that thoroughness often resolves.[186]
—Elizabeth Shown Mills

Negative Findings

When you search fruitlessly, do not be discouraged,
for progress is being made. Every record searched is a
record that no longer has to be searched.[187]
—*Lee Albright and Helen F. M. Leary*

When a genealogist continually finds
negative results, ... she's searching for
the wrong thing, time, place, or person.[188]
—*Stefani Evans*

Note Taking

Imagine that the original document will
disappear and only your abstract will survive.[189]
—*Duncan B. Gardiner*

Origins

//

The best clues to
a person's origin and birth family
are usually found in
the earliest proved place of
residence—even if that place is a
burned county.[190]
—Elizabeth Shown Mills

//

Photographs

A family photograph collection
is more than a random
collection of images;
each one is
a story worth saving.[191]
—*Maureen A. Taylor*

Plagiarism

Plagiarism:
Stealing a ride on
someone else's train of thought.[192]
—*Russell E. Curran*

Keep your hands from
literary picking and stealing.
But if you cannot refrain from
this kind of stealth,
abstain from murdering
what you steal.[193]
—*Augustus Toplady*

Plagiarism:
Larding your lean work
with the fat of others.[194]
—*Robert Burton*

Plagiarism:
The highest form of compliment
and the lowest form of larceny. —*Anonymous*

**Plagiarism is the line no writer can cross,
and if it is crossed, must be dealt with firmly.[195]
—*Nora Roberts***

Poor Folks

You never had to be famous, rich, or educated to leave a trace, but unless you were, you tended to be overlooked. Now, that's changing—and at the vanguard of this democraticization of history is the humble genealogist.[196]

—*Megan Smolenyak Smolenyak*

Poor [folks] do not make many historical registers unless we knock some rich man off his horse.[197]
—Rick Bragg

Whether our ancestor was poor or rich, he still had to associate with people. When we fail to find a record he created, that conveniently states where he came from, our best strategy is to study his neighbors and associates. Their records will usually lead us back to his family and origins.[198]

—*Elizabeth Shown Mills*

Privacy

The dead have no right to privacy.
That has been settled in court.
But they and their survivors are due respect.[199]
—*Debbie Mieszala*

||||||||||||||||||||||||||||||||||||||||||||||||||||||||||||||||||||||||||||

Genealogists seek truth,
but they are mindful of repercussions
from revealing it.[200]
—*Melinde Lutz Byrne & Thomas W. Jones*

Problem
Solving

**Genius is not so much a matter of
making great discoveries.
It's seeing the connections
between small things.**
—Anonymous

The most common cause of stalemates in Southern research is a tendency to conduct *look ups* rather than *investigations*. Pressed for time, researchers seek short-cuts. They typically search for the specific name of the key individual and limit themselves to indexed records. When that basic *look up* fails to yield an answer, many are temped to *give up*—blaming meager results on "poor recordkeeping" or "record destruction."[201]
—Rachal Mills Lennon

It's not just what a record *says* that solves a problem.
It's what we do with what we find.[202]
—Elizabeth Shown Mills

Problem Solving ⟶

Let there be no illusions:
Southern genealogy is difficult—
especially in remote areas and among "plain folk"
who resisted paper trails as fiercely as they did
meddling governments.[203]
—*Rachal Mills Lennon*

One of the great joys in life
is doing what other people
say you can't.
—Anonymous

Genealogical problems are not solved by
just finding sources that provide data. Many
sources err. Or, we may never find a source
that specifically states the information we
seek. Solutions to tough research problems are
thoughtfully and analytically constructed.[204]

—*Elizabeth Shown Mills*

Professional Genealogy

Clients are in control of the budget, but
ancestors are in control of the records.[205]
—*Elissa Scalise Powell*

[Professional] genealogists have methodological skills
that take years to perfect, and this creates our most
sustainable role. The client may cut down on [our]
actual research time by exhausting the usual suspects,
but a new perspective and viewpoint may find items
that the untrained eye could not see.[206]
—*Darcie M. Hind Posz*

**Your work is going to fill a large part of
your life, and the only way to be truly
satisfied is to do what you believe is great
work. And the only way to do great work is
to love what you do.[207]
—*Steve Jobs***

A genetic genealogist must consider the emotional
implications of DNA findings. When DNA tests
provide information a family may not want to believe,
the genealogist must lay a foundation to encourage its
acceptance.[208] —*Debbie Parker Wayne*

Professional Genealogy

If a single aspect of the proof standard remains unmet, our conclusion cannot be considered sufficiently proved. The professional should honestly communicate this to clients, both before and after the research has been conducted.[209]

—Michael G. Hait

Digitization [means that] demands for genealogical research will shift gears to become more customer service driven. Online databases already have that instant appeal, but an abundance of documentation will still need to be analyzed by a trained eye.[210] *—Darcie M. Hind Posz*

Create a demand
and then supply it well.[211]
—Elissa Scalise Powell

Genealogy is personal before it is anything else. People who enter other professions—physics, law, history—also start with simpler motivations, but these scholarly professions aren't rooted so deeply in personal soil.[212]

—Harold Henderson

⤙Professional Genealogy

Professional genealogy is not a product-based
industry. It is a time-based profession.
We don't make widgets or produce documents.
We analyze problems, seek evidence, and
evaluate findings. What clients buy is not just a
physical product but the knowledge and skills
between the researcher's ears.[213]
—*Elissa Scalise Powell*

||||||||||||||||||||||||||||||||||||||||||||||||||||||||||||||||

As genealogical professionals, we are expected to
know all the records that exist for the time, place,
and social group in which we work. We are expected
to know the laws and the legal language. We need
to understand the society and the ways in which
cultural heritage may have prompted forebears to
ignore the civil laws. We need to understand DNA
testing and how it can be used to resolve genealogical
questions. Above all, we have to understand what
constitutes valid proof of identity, kinship, and
other related matters.[214]
—*Elizabeth Shown Mills*

Proof

History offers no certainties. All it offers are
relics for us to analyze and interpret. That,
then, becomes the "proof" we offer
to support our own assertions.[215]
—*Elizabeth Shown Mills*

Trust no record in isolation.[216]
—Thomas W. Jones

Responsible genealogy does not form a
thesis first and find evidence to support it.
Responsible genealogy looks at the evidence
and forms a conclusion based on facts.[217]
—*Helen F. M. Leary*

One does not convince a jury by
presenting only one piece of evidence.
It is the sum of the evidence that
creates the proof.[218]
—***Barbara Vines Little***

Proof

Research questions can never be considered closed and must always be reconsidered should new evidence be found.[219] —*Donn Devine*

Never settle for a single source that seems to provide the answer to the research question. Any given source can be wrong. Even when direct evidence exists, always look for evidence in other sources to corroborate or contradict it.[220]
—*Laura Murphy DeGrazia*

Even when we find records for a person of the "right" name in the right time and place, we still must establish that the record relates to our person and not someone else of the same name.[221]
—Elizabeth Shown Mills

Proof⟶

Proof is not a source or a citation. It is a body of evidence accumulated in the process of research and analysis. Individual sources provide assertions. Researchers still must assemble a body of evidence to satisfy reasonable doubts that each and every assertion is reliable and that each pertains to the specific individual under study.[222]
—*Elizabeth Shown Mills*

> It's not what you know.
> It's what you can prove.[223]
> —"Alonzo Harris"

A conclusion ... is often called "proof,"
but the best we can actually achieve
is an answer with a high degree of credibility,
explained in words that will convince
most reasonable people that it is actual fact.[224]
—*Donn Devine*

Sources provide information from which
we identify evidence for analysis.
A sound conclusion may then be considered proof.[225]
—*Elizabeth Shown Mills*

When we apply a proof standard to others' findings, we minimize the risk of polluting our sound research with their dubious conclusions.[226]
—*Thomas W. Jones*

Our goal is to prove our conclusions. While we are researching, proof is just a target. We do not achieve proof—we do not hit the target—until we complete the research, evaluate and assemble the evidence, resolve any conflicts, explain our conclusions in writing, and share with others.[227] —*Thomas W. Jones*

> **Proof is a fundamental concept in genealogy. In order to merit confidence, each conclusion about an ancestor must have sufficient credibility to be accepted as "proved." Acceptable conclusions, therefore, meet the Genealogical Proof Standard.[228]**
> —*Elissa Scalise Powell*

You can't force a 'proof.'[229]
—Tony Proctor

The word "proof" is just shorthand for
"At this point, the weight of the evidence
points to a conclusion that ..."[230]
—*Elizabeth Shown Mills*

Our citations tell readers exactly what we used and whether or not our conclusions and claims of proof rest on likely accurate sources.[231]
—*Thomas W. Jones*

Proof Statements

Organizing pieces of evidence and writing up a statement of proof will help us spot missing pieces or find the fallacy in our argument.[232]

—*Barbara Vines Little*

Quality

Excellence is not measured by how well you do something, but how consistently you do it.[233]

—*Diana Crisman Smith*

Questions

Any one record can generate a
million questions, but the most
important question is this: How
accurate is the information?[234]

—*Dee Parmer Woodtor*

Reasonably Exhaustive Research

Reasonably exhaustive research—
the most common cause
of former ancestors![235]
—Yvette Hoitink

Any unexamined record is a ticking time bomb
likely to explode our premature conclusion.[236]
—*Elizabeth Shown Mills*

Effective family historians consult and access all sources, regardless of type, that might help answer their research questions. They exclude no potentially useful source, and they trust no unverified source.[237]
—*Thomas W. Jones*

Reasonably Exhaustive Research

Novice genealogists create their own "brick walls"
by not locating all the records that may be
relevant to the research question and ultimately
missing those needed to solve the problem.[238]
—*Angela Packer McGhie*

Do not consider the research complete if the person
being pursued is not yet placed in the context of family,
community, and time.[239] —*David McDonald*

Ease of access
is not the determining factor when
considering what sources we use.[240]
—Michael G. Hait

DNA evidence is among the types of evidence a
knowledgeable researcher would seek, and so it is
within the scope of the reasonably exhaustive search,
if suitable donors can be identified and consent
to testing. If none can be found, the "reasonably
exhaustive search" requirement has been satisfied, and
the paper evidence can stand on its own.[241]

—*Donn Devine*

Records

Few documents are created in isolation and the context of any document consists of all the parts, not a single item. Thus, we ask the question: What other records were created because of this record?[242]

—*Barbara Vines Little*

|||||||||||||||||||||||||||||||||||||||||||||||||||||||||||||||||||||||||||||||||||||||||||||||||||||||||

For every piece of paper created, there is another piece of paper created in reaction to that piece.[243]

—Craig R. Scott

|||||||||||||||||||||||||||||||||||||||||||||||||||||||||||||||||||||||||||||||||||||||||||||||||||||||||

Research

**Research is not a matter of
looking up the answer,
but of tracking down the answer.**[244]
—Sarah Larsen

Finding random documents
to support what we want to believe
is not research. It's self-delusion.[245]
—Elizabeth Shown Mills

Research is not trolling the Internet for
names of interest. Research is not using
indexes and database entries as though
they were actual records. Research is not
accepting uncritically whatever conclusions
others assert. What research *is* is a three-
stage circular process that consists of
preparation, performance, and reporting.[246]
—Elizabeth Shown Mills

Every [research] step
involves two distinct activities:
One is the search and
the other is the analysis.[247]
—Dee Parmer Woodtor

Research

**A research plan
is my road map to research.**[248]
—Elissa Scalise Powell

Hope
is not a strategy.[249]
—Rick Page

A researcher is not just a collector of "facts."
A researcher is an analyst and
an interpreter of those facts.[250]
—Elizabeth Shown Mills

**Research can never be considered
closed and must always be reconsidered
should new evidence be found.**[251]
—Donn Devine

Succeful research is reliable research. It's not a big
tree or a long line back to Charlemagne. Success is
measured by whether our research withstands efforts
to disprove it.[252] —Elizabeth Shown Mills

When we find a record, we should—right then, right there—extract and analyze all details. If we do grab-and-go genealogy, copying a mass of documents with plans to process it all later, what we will discover later is that we wasted much of our time because some detail in one of those records should have sent us in a new direction.[253] —*Elizabeth Shown Mills*

There are two newspaper search methods: the shotgun approach and the rifle approach. In the shotgun approach, you use online databases to broadly search digitized news-papers. The rifle approach uses online sources to determine if copies of historical newspapers still exist for the location and time period.[254]
—*Barbara Renick*

It does not matter whether our ancestor was poor or rich. He still had to associate with people. When we fail to find a record he created, that conveniently states where he came from, our best strategy is to study his neighbors and associates. Their records will usually lead us back to his family and origins.[255]
—*Elizabeth Shown Mills*

Research

> What we absolutely, positively
> should not try is the shotgun
> approach—looking willy-nilly,
> hither and yon, for somebody,
> anybody, of the "right" name.[256]
>
> —*Elizabeth Shown Mills*

> "Google"
> is not a synonym for
> "research."[257]
> —Dan Brown

A human life is a chain—a chain of people, events, and patterns of behavior. We may pick up our ancestor at any point on this life chain. Whether we move forward or backward in time, he is still part of this continuous chain and the life we reconstruct for him, as we attempt to track him, must have human, social, economic, and religious links. There will be those links, if we have assembled that life correctly.[258]

> —*Elizabeth Shown Mills*

(The) Research
Question

**The first step is to decide
what your research question is
—a clear definition of the scope
of your investigation is the most
important factor in designing a
sound plan for carrying it out.**[259]
*—Lee Albright and
Helen F. M. Leary*

Without a research question,
genealogical evidence
does not exist.[260]
—Thomas W. Jones

Research
Traps

Beware of "the only one"![261]
—*Elizabeth Shown Mills*

||||||||||||||||||||||||||||

Trap:
Going back too far too fast.
Once genealogists find new ancestors,
they immediately want to search for parents
instead of learning as much as they can
about the new ancestors.[262]
—*Tony Burroughs*

Roots

Mus tek cyear a de root fal heal de tree.
(You must nurture the root to heal the tree.)[263]
—*Marquetta L. Goodwine*

There are only two lasting bequests we
can hope to give our children—
one is roots, the other, wings.[264]
—Hodding S. Carter

Silence

Troubled silence is a part of the African American collective memory: silence about specific events, silence about ancestry, ... and even selective "dis-remembering" of ancestry.[265]   —*Dee Parmer Woodtor*

"You have no ancestry! ... Look up, not down. Look forward, not back. Look to the future, not the past!" Such remarks, frequently made to me in my youth by my own father, illustrate a common attitude among older African-Americans. ... Not a single story, not a single tradition about slavery, ever filtered down to [me]. ... Perhaps denial was a way of forgetting unpleasant experiences.[266]
—*Rev. C. Bernard Ruffin III*

I sometimes think that my parents' generation, like the generations before them, had been trained to keep silence so well that they had lost the ability to even think such questions were permissible.[267]
—*Dee Parmer Woodtor*

Software

Genealogy programs allow users to record numerous facts. However, the Genealogical Proof Standard requires genealogists to conduct thorough research for all relevant information and knowledgeably analyze all evidence before reaching a conclusion [about each "fact"]. Until research has met all of the proof standard's conditions, a genealogist cannot consider any conclusion proved.[268]

—*Michael G. Hait*

Solutions

Whenever a problem arises, the solution

... lies in our approach. We have to make

a new approach that was not

followed by others before.

The way we see the problem

is the problem.

—Stephen R. Covey et al.[269]

Sources

Those who devote themselves solely
to the printed word do not understand
what genealogical research
is all about.[270]
—*Val D. Greenwood*

**Some source types have higher error rates
than others, but no type is error-free or
worthless.[271] —*Thomas W. Jones***

The phrases "primary sources' and
"secondary sources" have always been
rough approximations in most scholarly
use, more as a categorization tool rather
than a truly meaningful definition.[272]
—*Christopher Candy*

Effective family historians consult and access all
sources, regardless of type, that might help answer
their research questions. They exclude no potentially
useful source, and they trust no unverified source.[273]
—*Thomas W. Jones*

Sources

> Good intentions to go to the best source
> do not substitute for actually doing it.[274]
> —*Stefani Evans*

> When you drink from the water,
> consider the source.
> —American Folk Saying

> A source's accuracy is unknown until the
> researcher has accumulated enough evidence
> for tests of correlation—the comparison and
> contrasting of sources and information to reveal
> points of agreement and disagreement.[275]
> —*Thomas W. Jones*

Standards

Using standards does not mean that
genealogists become clones.[276]
—*Donald J. Mosemann*

I refuse to lower my standards
to accommodate those who
refuse to raise theirs.[277]
—*Steve Gamlin*

**The road to genealogy's standing
as a serious and respected profession
lies through the acceptance of standards.[278]
—*Michael Ramage***

Just as standards apply when driving a car
(stopping for a red light or keeping to the
appropriate side of a road), genealogical
standards bring order and help prevent
kinship "accidents" such as attaching the
wrong people to our family tree.[279]
—*Elissa Scalise Powell*

When we use sources from fields in which we are not
"expert," we don't suspend our own standards. Acceptable
works from other fields should meet the same standards
we demand in genealogy.[280]
—*Elizabeth Shown Mills*

Stories & Storytelling

The most erroneous stories are those we think we know best—and therefore never scrutinize or question. [281]
—Stephen Jay Gould

We are the chosen ones. In each family there is one who seems called to find the ancestors. To put flesh on their bones and make them live again. To tell of their family story and to feel that somehow they know and approve. Doing genealogy is not a cold gathering of facts but, instead, breathing life into all who have gone before. We are the story tellers of the tribe. All tribes have one. We have been called by those who have gone before.[282]
—Della M. Cummings Wright

Storytelling is the oldest form of education. Stories are the way our brains most easily store and retrieve information. And stories are easy to remember because they put the information into the context of the listener's own life and experiences.[283]
—Judy G. Russell

Stories & Storytelling

People are hungry for stories.
It's part of our very being.
Storytelling is a form of history,
of immortality too.
It goes from one generation to another.[284]
—*Studs Terkel*

||||||||||||||||||||||||||||||||||

If you don't recount your family history,
it will be lost.
Honor your own stories and tell them too.
The tales may not seem very important,
but they are what binds families
and makes each of us who we are.[285]
—*Madeleine L'Engle*

Success

Professional genealogists are
responsible for the skills.
Clients control the budget.
Ancestors control the records.
Successful research happens at the
intersection of these three.[286]
—Elissa Scalise Powell

We cannot create records,
but success comes to those
who use records creatively.[287]
—Elizabeth Shown Mills

Successful use of DNA tests requires understanding
how to interpret the tests and how to use the tools.[288]
—Elizabeth Shown Mills

Tax Records

The value of tax records is significantly leveraged [by] comparing the changes over a period of time. If the records are not in alphabetical order, be sure to record the names of the neighbors for ten to twelve lines in each direction.[289]
—*David E. Rencher*

A lot of evidence lies in the spaces between records. Using tax lists as an example, one can witness the descendancy of land through the generations by noting the acreage taxed [to] people over a long period of time. This evidence is certainly based on a series of records, but the whole is far greater than the sum of the facts.[290]
—*Michael G. Hait*

Teaching

Give a person their family tree
and they will hang it on their wall.
Teach a person how to research and
they will cherish their heritage forever.[291]
—*A. C. Ivory*

When one teaches, two learn.[292]
—*Robert Heinlein*

You can tell someone how to do
something. You can show them how to
do something. Neither one is the same
as knowing how to do something.
What lives in that gap is experience.[293]
—Melinde Lutz Byrne

Traditions

Family histories are a series of myths, embellished and perpetuated through gossamer tales retold over the Thanksgiving turkey. They are blandly reassuring, these myths, they give us the illusion that we know from whence we came without forcing upon us the details that make real life so perfectly vulgar.[294]   —*William Lashner*

Traditions of origin of most of the prominent Gambian Mandinka lineages tend to be bodies of myth containing small, but often recognizable, skeletons of historical truth.[295]
—*Donald R. Wright*

There is no such thing as
The Gospel According to Grandma.[296]
—*Elizabeth Shown Mills*

Folklore, when money is involved, is often fakelore.[297]
—*Elizabeth Shown Mills*

Just because it is said does not make it true.
Just because it cannot be found does not make it false.[298]
—*James Walton*

Traditions

The first and best rule is this: Proceed to research the family as if the Indian tradition did not exist. As the ancestral lines of the presumed Indian are extended back, a Native American connection (or clues to one) could surface in any type of record.[299]

—*Rachal Mills Lennon*

Trivial Details

> The records we use are filled with
> "trivia," bits and pieces of data that
> seem to have no "genealogical value."
> Each piece of trivia in every document
> is an opportunity waiting to be
> connected to something else.
> Our ability to resolve problems
> depends upon our ability
> to make those connections.[300]
>
> —*Elizabeth Shown Mills*

Trust

In God we trust.
All others must show sources.[301]

—*David Woody*

Genealogists consult everything
and trust nothing.[302]
—Thomas W. Jones

**Don't trust everything you see.
Even salt looks like sugar.
—*American Folk Saying***

If you rely on incorrect information, you will spend
money researching ancestors who are not yours.[303]
—*Jan Alpert*

It's in our biology to trust what we see with our eyes.
This makes living in a carefully edited, overproduced,
and Photoshopped world very dangerous.[304]
—*Brené Brown*

Truth

Most issues in life come down to particles of truth wrapped in different points of view.[305] —*David Clapp*

In seeking truth
you have to get both sides of a story.[306]
—*Walter Kronkite*

Memory is a complicated thing,
a relative to truth.[307]
—*Barbara Kingsolver*

The past was real,
but truth is relative.[308]
—Robert Winks

We depend upon records to reveal the "truth" about
the past. Yet records have anomalies. Some are
amusing or humorous. Some are interesting or weird.
Some are peculiar or suspicious. Some are infuriating
or downright laughable.
Records say the darnedest things![309]
—*Robert Raymond*

Truth ⟶

You shall know the truth,
and the truth shall make you mad.[310]
—Alduous Huxley

The truth does not change according to
our ability to stomach it.[311]
—*Flannery O'Connor*

**Genealogists seek truth,
but they are mindful of
repercussions from revealing it.[312]
—*Melinde Lutz Byrne & Thomas W. Jones***

A genetic genealogist must consider the
emotional implications of DNA findings.
When DNA tests provide information
a family may not want to believe, the
genealogist must lay a foundation to
encourage its acceptance.[313]
—*Debbie Parker Wayne*

Never be ashamed of the truth or of your ancestors.
After all, who knows how they might feel about you![314]
—*Val D. Greenwood*

Uncertainty

I can live with doubt and uncertainty
and not knowing.
I think it's much more interesting to live
not knowing than to have answers
which might be wrong.

—Richard Feynman[315]

Understanding

People have reasons for doing what they do. That reason, if we can find it, usually provides information we can use.[316]
—*Stefani Evans*

Whether using a database or a document, the crucial question the researcher must ask is not "What does this say?" but "What does this mean?"[317]
—GeLee Corley Hendrix

When we find something we don't understand, it's a bone we need to gnaw at until we crack it.[318]
—*Elizabeth Shown Mills*

One who is ignorant of geography cannot know history.[319]
—*Max Anders*

Failure to understand the context of a document can lead to false assumptions.[320] —*Barbara Vines Little*

War

**My ancestors fought in every war.
Apparently they couldn't
get along with anyone!**
—Anonymous

Every war fought on American soil
brought death, theft, and wanton
destruction to the doorsteps of helpless
families. Yet each also gave birth to a
wealth of records descendants can use to
recreate ancestral lives.[321]
—*Elizabeth Shown Mills*

Wars by their nature create paper—
an enormous volume of paper.
The aftermath of war creates
even more paper.[322]
—Craig R. Scott

Writing

The disciplined thought that writing requires can result in saving more time than the writing required.[323]
—Donn Devine

The beauty of writing is that it helps us clarify our thoughts. The frustration of writing is that it forces us to clarify our thoughts.[324]   *—Elizabeth Shown Mills*

A writer who waits for ideal conditions under which to work will die without putting a word on paper.[325]
—E. B. White

**I write because I don't know what I think until I read what I say.[326]
*—Flannery O'Connor***

The best writers can't disguise sloppy or shallow research. And good research will shine through awkward sentences and misplaced commas. But a well-edited presentation can make excellent research sing.[327]   *—Stefani Evans*

Genealogists who produce a family narrative must use words to recreate the historical context in which their ancestors actually lived. Be careful what words you use. Understanding the physical and social world of a bygone time in a bygone place, and representing that world in writing, are challenging tasks.[328]

—John Philip Colletta

The Two Basic Rules of Family History Writing:
1. **Do not 'wait until I finish my research' to get started. You will never finish your research.**
2. **Do not try to tell everyone everything. You will become overwhelmed and lose your motivation.**[329]

—Linda Coffin

Written words can sit on paper (or a computer screen) until you are sure they are perfect—and you should be sure they are perfect before submitting or printing. Let them marinate for a few days, hours, or minutes (depending on your deadline) before finalizing.[330]

—Diana Crisman Smith

As genealogists, our writing has two objectives: to convey facts accurately and clearly, and to convey them interestingly so that our families will enjoy and appreciate the work we have done.[331]

—Elizabeth Shown Mills

Writing

Compelling writing lives in the
blank spaces. It's about learning
to say the most with the fewest words.
Make each word have
weight and importance,
and realize what you leave out
is just as powerful sometimes
as what you leave in.[332]
—*Clay Mills*

References

1. Dee Parmer Woodtor, *Finding a Place Called Home: A Guide to African-American Genealogy and Historical Identity* (New York: Random House, 1999), 71.

2. Thomas W. Jones, "Perils of Source Snobbery," *OnBoard: Newsletter of the Board for Certification of Genealogists* 18 (May 2012): 10.

3. Joe Moore, *Have You Ever Noticed* (New York: Pocket Books, 1988), dedication page.

4. Val D. Greenwood, *The Researcher's Guide to American Genealogy*, 3rd ed. (Baltimore: Genealogical Publishing Co., 2000), 10.

5. GeLee Corley Hendrix, "Going Beyond the Database: Interpretation, Amplification, and Development of Evidence —South Carolina's COM Index and Several James Kellys," *National Genealogical Society Quarterly* 86 (June 1998): 133.

6. Debra Newman Carter, comment, 29 September 2016, at "Elizabeth Shown Mills," personal page, *Facebook* (https://www.facebook.com/elizabeth.shownmills : posted 29 September 2016).

7. "Unusually," *Fine Dictionary* (http://www.finedictionary.com/unusually.html : accessed 15 January 2017).

8. Woodtor, *Finding a Place Called Home,* 249.

9. Stephen Jay Gould, *Full House: The Spread of Excellence from Plato to Darwin* (New York: Harmony Books, 1997), 30.

10. Dennis B. Neuenschwander, "Bridges and Eternal Keepsakes," *The Church of Jesus Christ of Latter-day Saints, General Conference* (https://www.lds.org/general-conference/1999/04/bridges-and-eternal-keepsakes?lang=eng : posted April 1999; accessed 15 October 2016).

References

11. Roshni Mooneeram, "We Stand Tall Today Because We Stand on the Shoulders of Our Ancestors: Amika Dwarka, the Silent Lightworker," *LeMauricien: Indépendant d'information et d'opinion* (http://www.lemauricien.com/arti cle/we-stand-tall-today-because-we-stand-shoulders-our-ancestors-amika-dwarka-silent-lightworker : posted 29 December 2015; accessed 15 October 2016).

12. Bill Rodman, *The Spirit of a Culture: Cane River Creoles*, documentary (Natchitoches: Louisiana Public Broadcasting, 2005), Louis Metoyer interview, hour: minute 1: 14.

13. Plutarch, *Moralia,* vol. 8; quoted in *The Columbia Dictionary of Quotations* (New York: Columbia University Press, 1993), 39.

14. Jean Baptiste Poquelin alias Molière (1622–1673), quoted in Rhoda Thomas Tripp, *The International Thesaurus of Quotations* (New York: Thomas Y. Crowell, 1970), 37.

15. Benvenuto Cellini, *Autobiography (1558–66),* quoted in ibid., 37.

16. Thomas Fuller, *Gnomologia: Adagies and Proverbs, Wise Sentences and Witty Sayings, Ancient and Modern, Foreign and British* (London: B. Barker, 1732), 86, quote 2144.

17. Elder Russel M. Nelson, quoted in "Family History Work Vital, Prophets and Apostles Say," *The Church of Jesus Christ of Latter-day Saints* (https://www.lds.org/prophets -and-apostles/unto-all-the-world/family-history-work-vital -prophets-and-apostles-say?lang=eng : accessed 15 October 2016).

18. "Topics in Brief," *The Literary Digest* 70 (16 July 1921), 15; crediting the *Minneapolis Tribune.*

19. Attributed to Abraham Lincoln by numerous sources such as Michael Kammen, *Mystic Chords of Memory: The Transformation of Tradition in American Culture* (1991; re-

print New York: Vintage Books, 1993), 221. The quote is not among the confirmed Lincoln quotes (drawn from speeches only) at Roy P. Basler et al., "Selected Quotations by Abraham Lincoln," *Abraham Lincoln Online: Speeches & Writings* (www.abrahamlincolnonline.org/lincoln/speeches/quotes .htm : accessed 15 October 2016).

20. Oliver Wendell Holmes I, quoted in Eugene E. Brussell, *Webster's New World Dictionary of Quotable Definitions*, 2nd ed. (New York: Webster's New World, 1988), 254.

21. Helen Keller, *The Story of My Life* (1954; reprinted, Minneola, N.Y.: Dover Publications, 1996), 1.

22. "Lord Illingworth" to "Gerald Arbuthnot," in Oscar Wilde, "A Woman of No Importance," act 3; archived at *Full-Books* (http://www.fullbooks.com/A-Woman-of-No-Importance2.html : accessed 27 August 2016).

23. Greenwood, *Researcher's Guide to American Genealogy*, 12.

24. Megan Smolenyak Smolenyak to E. S. Mills, email, 25 August 2016.

25. Tony Burroughs, "Why Retracing Our African Roots Is So Difficult," guest blog, *Anderson Cooper's AC360* (http:// ac360.blogs.cnn.com/2009/07/17/why-re-tracing-our-afri can-roots-is-so-difficult: posted 17 July 2009; accessed 27 August 2016).

26. E. S. Mills, "7 Ways to Jumpstart Your Research," session T–238, 8 June 2006, National Genealogical Society annual conference, Chicago, Ill.

27. Michael D. Lacopo, "How to Overcome Brick Walls in Pennsylvania Research," Federation of Genealogical Societies, *Time Travel: Centuries of Memories*, annual conference syllabus (Austin, Tex.: FGS, 2016), 212.

References

28. Attributed to Jennifer Aniston by many quotation sites without details of time, place, and circumstances; for example, see "The 30 Most Empowering Jennifer Aniston Quotes Ever," *Feeling Success* (https://www.feelingsuccess.com/30 -jennifer-aniston-quotes/ : accessed 15 October 2016).

29. Richard Bach, *Illusions: The Adventures of a Reluctant Messiah* (New York: Delta/Random House, 1977), 134.

30. Angela Packer McGhie, "What Happens When We Do Not Follow Standards?" *Association of Professional Genealogists Quarterly* 28 (December 2013): 177.

31. E. S. Mills, "Problem-Solving in the Problem-Riddled Carolina Backcountry," presentation, National Genealogical Society annual conference, Charleston, S.C., 11–14 May 2011, session F327.

32. Attributed to Florence Nightingale, at University of California–Los Angeles, Statistics Online Computational Resource, *SOCR Quotes* (http://wiki.stat.ucla.edu/socr/index. php/SOCR_Quotes : accessed 20 October 2016).

33. Edgar E. McDonald, "Richard Sayre's November 7 Slatten Lectures," Friends of the Virginia State Archives, *Archives News* 19 (Summer 2009): 10.

34. Harold Henderson, "Indecision as a Genealogical Virtue," *Archives* (www.Archives.com/experts/henderson-har old/indecision-as-a-genealogical-virtue.html : posted 25 June 2013; accessed 15 October 2016).

35. L. P. Hartley, *The Go-Between* (1941; reprint, New York: New York Review of Books, 2002), 17.

36. Wayne C. Booth, Gregory G. Colomb, and Joseph M. Williams, *The Craft of Research,* 3rd ed. (Chicago: University of Chicago Press, 2008), 119.

37. E. S. Mills, "Censuses: Analysis, Interpretation & Correlation," Advanced Research Methodology & Evidence Analy-

sis track, 1986–2013, Samford University Institute of Genealogy and Historical Research (IGHR), Birmingham, Ala.

38. Woodtor, *Finding a Place Called Home,* 131.

39. "David Foster Wallace in His Own Words ... 2005 Commencement Address at Kenyon College," *The Economist 1843* (https://www.1843magazine.com/story/david-foster-wallace-in-his-own-words : posted 19 September 2008; accessed 26 November 2016), para. 6.

40. Thomas W. Jones, "Maximizing Your Use of Evidence," National Genealogical Society, *Follow Your Ancestral Trail,* annual conference syllabus (Arlington, Va.: NGS, 2010), 352.

41. Alison Hare, "Building Better Citations," National Genealogical Society, *Where the Past Is Still Present,* annual conference syllabus (Arlington, Va.: NGS, 2011), 457.

42. Adapted from Thomas W. Jones, *Mastering Genealogical Proof* (Arlington, Va.: National Genealogical Society, 2013), 33, 36.

43. Jones, "Maximizing Your Use of Evidence," 352.

44. E. S. Mills, *QuickSheet: The Historical Biographer's Guide to the Research Process,* 1st ed. rev. (Baltimore: Genealogical Publishing Co., 2017), leaf4.

45. Carol Baxter, "Help! Historical and Genealogical Truth: How Do I Separate Fact from Fiction?" Federation of Genealogical Societies, *Time Travel: Centuries of Memories,* annual conference syllabus (Austin, Tex.: FGS, 2016), 196.

46. Elissa Scalise Powell, "Beating the Bushes: Finding Jacob Bush's Father; A Case Study in Correlation of Records Using the GPS," National Genealogical Society, *Follow Your Ancestral Trail,* annual conference syllabus (Arlington, Va.: NGS, 2010), 408.

47. Thomas W. Jones, "When Sources Don't Agree, Then What?" National Genealogical Society, *Where the Past Is*

References

Still Present, annual conference syllabus (Arlington, Va.: NGS, 2011), 37.

48. Adapted from Alison Hare, "The Time of Cholera: A Case Study about Historical Context," in National Genealogical Society, *Where the Past Is Still Present,* annual conference syllabus (Arlington, Va.: NGS, 2011), 379.

49. David McDonald, "Top Ten Tips to Concluding Effective Research," session S-451, 14 May 2011, National Genealogical Society annual conference, Charleston, S.C.

50. Barbara Vines Little, "Working with Documents: The Importance of Context in Record Analysis," National Genealogical Society, *Virginia: The First Frontier,* annual conference syllabus (Arlington, Va.: NGS, 2014), 477–78.

51. E. S. Mills, "Finding & Using Birth, Marriage & Death Records Prior to Vital Registration," National Genealogical Society, *Follow Your Ancestral Trail,* annual conference syllabus (Arlington, Va.: NGS, 2010), 495.

52. Paul K. Graham, "Certification, Accreditation, and the Genealogy Career," *Association of Professional Genealogists Quarterly* 28 (June 2013): 80.

53. Claude Bernard, *Experimental Medicine,* Henry Copley Greene, transl., introduction by Stewart Wolf (1926; reprint, New Brunswick, N.J.: Transaction Publishers, 1999), 222.

54. René Magritte, quoted in Adrianne Marcus, *Magritte's Stones* (N.P.: Winepress Services, 2001), 24, citing "Unscripted interview, 1964–5, with Jean Neyens."

55. Thomas W. Jones, *Mastering Genealogical Documentation* (Arlington, Va.: National Genealogical Society, 2017), 12.

56. David Woody, *RootsWeb Review,* 2: 17, 28 April 1999.

57. Pamela K. Sayer, "Effective Editing & Writing," National Genealogical Society, *Follow Your Ancestral Trail,* annual conference syllabus (Arlington, Va.: NGS, 2010), 454.

58. E. S. Mills, "Edit Yourself," presentation, Genealogy as a Profession track, 1992–95, Samford University IGHR.

59. Elissa Scalise Powell, invoked everywhere.

60. E. S. Mills, "Finding Fathers: Bridging the Generation Gap," session S-401, 24 August 2013, National Genealogical Society annual conference, Fort Wayne, Ind.

61. Robert Charles Anderson, "Documenting New England's Founders in the Great Migration Directory," *American Ancestors* 16 (Spring 2015): 27.

62. Michael John Neill, *Genealogy Tip of the Day* (http://genealogytipoftheday.blogspot.com/ : posted 13 August 2012); this "tip" is not currently found at the site, in the wake of a reorganization.

63. Roger D. Joslyn to E. S. Mills, email, 19 August 2016, describing his advice to fellow researchers.

64. Judy G. Russell, "DNA and the Golden Rule: The Law and Ethics of Genetic Genealogy," National Genealogical Society, *Virginia: The First Frontier,* annual conference syllabus (Arlington, Va.: NGS, 2014), 477–78.

65. Paula Stuart-Warren, "Native American Research: Keys to Success," National Genealogical Society, *The Ohio River: Gateway to the Western Frontier,* annual conference syllabus (Arlington, Va.: NGS, 2012), 59.

66. Burroughs, *Black Roots,* 35.

67. Woodtor, *Finding a Place Called Home,* 14.

68. Nancy Richey, "I Don't Even Know My Name: Researching African American Roots," National Genealogical Society, *Where the Past Is Still Present,* annual conference syllabus (Arlington, Va.: NGS, 2011), 469.

69. Burroughs, *Black Roots,* 34.

70. Woodtor, *Finding a Place Called Home,* 10.

References

71. Terrel A. Delphin, Tracey Colson Fontenot, and Lair LaCour, variously expressed throughout Bill Rodman, *The Spirit of a Culture: Cane River Creoles,* documentary (Natchitoches: Louisiana Public Broadcasting, 2005).

72. Gary Mokotoff, email to E. S. Mills, 16 August 2016, quoting his most frequent advice to Jewish researchers.

73. Rachal Mills Lennon, *Tracing Ancestors among the Five Civilized Tribes* (Baltimore: Genealogical Publishing Co., 2002), 16.

74. Stuart-Warren, "Native American Research," 59.

75. Edward Tufte, *Beautiful Evidence* (Cheshire, Conn.: Graphics Press, 2006), 9; quoted by Margaret R. Fortier, "Visualizing Information for Client Reports," *Association of Professional Genealogists Quarterly* 29 (June 2014): 86.

76. Jones, "Maximizing Your Use of Evidence," 352.

77. Michael Hait, "Why I Do Not Use Genealogy Database Software," *Association of Professional Genealogists Quarterly* 34 [27] (September 2012): 153.

78. E. S. Mills, "QuickLesson 13: Classes of Evidence—Direct, Indirect, and Negative," *Evidence Explained: Historical Analysis, Citation & Source Usage* (https://www. evidenceexplained.com/content/quicklesson-13-classes-evidence-direct-indirect-negative : posted 1 November 2012).

79. Jones, "Maximizing Your Use of Evidence," 352.

80. Henry David Thoreau, *The Journal, 1837–1861* (various editions), under date 11 November 1854.

81. Adapted from Robert Raymond, "Frankenstein Genealogy," *The Ancestry Insider* (http://www.ancestryinsider.org /2011/03/frankenstein-genealogy.html : posted 23 March 2011; accessed 15 October 2016).

82. Edward George Earle Bulwer-Lytton (Lord Lytton),

References

"Some Observations on Shy People," in Edward A. Allen and William Schuyler, *The World's Best Essays from the Earliest Period to the Present Time,* Royal ed., 10 vols. (St. Louis: Ferdinand P. Kaiser, 1900), 7: 2709–10.

83. Anaïs Nin, *The Diary of Anaïs Nin, Volume 3, 1939– 1944,* Gunther Stuhlmann, ed. (New York: Harcourt, Brace, Jovanovich, 1971), 160.

84. Blaine Bettinger, "DNA and the Genealogical Proof Standard," Federation of Genealogical Societies, *Time Travel: Centuries of Memories,* annual conference syllabus (Austin, Tex.: FGS, 2016), 435.

85. Thomas W. Jones, "When Sources Don't Agree, Then What?" National Genealogical Society, *Where the Past Is Still Present,* annual conference syllabus (Arlington, Va.: NGS, 2011), 37.

86. Lewis Schiff, quoted in Vanessa Merit Nornberg, "Your Story Is Your Marketing Strategy," *Inc.* (http://www.inc.com/ vanessa-merit-nornberg/why-your-story-should-be-your-marketing-strategy.html : posted 25 May 2012; accessed 15 October 2016).

87. Marilynne Robinson, *Housekeeping: A Novel* (1980; reprint, New York: Macmillan/Picador, 2004), 217.

88. Extracted from Della M. Cummings Wright, "The Story Tellers," attribution and publication by the author's granddaughter Della Joann McGinnis Johnson, "Scribe of a Kansas History," *Genealogy.com* (www.genealogy.com/ftm/ m/c/g/Djmj-Mcginnis-Kansas/index.html : updated 5 January 2004; accessed 15 October 2016).

89. Charles Dickens, *The Personal History of David Copperfield,* 2 vols. (Boston: Houghton, Mifflin, 1894), 1: 420.

90. Gail Lumet Buckley, *The Hornes: An American Family* (New York: Applause Books, 1986), 4.

References

91. Jane Howard, *Families* (1978; reprint, New Brunswick, N.J.: Transaction Publishers, 1999), 234.

92. "Anthony Brandt," *Goodreads* (http://www.goodreads.com/author/show/202465.Anthony_Brandt : accessed 7 August 2016), "Quotes by Anthony Brandt."

93. E. S. Mills, posting on personal page, *Facebook* (https://www.facebook.com/elizabeth.shownmills : posted 27 March 2012).

94. Kelsey Grammer ("Frasier Crane") in "A Tsar Is Born," NBC, *Frasier,* 19 April 2001.

95. Megan Smolenyak Smolenyak to E. S. Mills, email, 25 August 2016.

96. E. S. Mills, *QuickSheeet: The Historical Biographer's Guide to Cluster Research—The FAN Principle,* 1st ed. rev. (Baltimore: Genealogical Publishing Co., 2017), leaf 1.

97. Rachal Mills Lennon, "Identifying a Son for John Temple of Virginia, Georgia, South Carolina, and Alabama," *National Geneaogical Society Quarterly* 103 (June 2015): 139.

98. Kay Haviland Freilich, "Research Strategies That Work," National Genealogical Society, *Virginia: The First Frontier,* annual conference syllabus (Arlington, Va.: NGS, 2014), 112.

99. Thomas W. Jones, "Proved? Five Ways to Prove Who Your Ancestor Was (Some Reliable and Others Not Reliable)," National Genealogical Society, *Follow Your Ancestral Trail,* annual conference syllabus (Arlington, Va.: NGS, 2010), 13.

100. Harold Henderson, review, "*Mind Maps for Genealogy: Enhanced Research Planning, Correlation, and Analysis,* by Ron Aarons," *National Genealogical Society Quarterly* 103 (June 2015): 156.

101. Powell, "Beating the Bushes," 408.

102. Thomas W. Jones, "The Genealogical Proof Standard (GPS): What It Is and What It Is Not," National Genealogical Society, *Where the Past Is Still Present,* annual conference syllabus (Arlington, Va.: NGS, 2011), 355.

103. Michael G. Hait, "Meeting the Genealogical Proof Standard in a Client Research Project," *Association of Professional Genealogists Quarterly* 28 (December 2013): 183.

104. Bettinger, "DNA and the Genealogical Proof Standard," 435.

105. Condensed from Hait, "Why I Do Not Use Genealogy Database Software," 153.

106. Attributed to John Garland Pollard, in Ashton Applewhite et al., *And I Quote: The Definitive Collection of Quotes, Sayings, and Jokes for the Contemporary Speech Maker* (New York: St. Martin's Press, 1992), 380.

107. *Board for Certification of Genealogists* (http://www. bcgcertification.org : accessed 15 October 2016), home page.

108. Senator Orrin Hatch, in his 2001 proposal to Congress to create Family History Month; cited by Alexandria Edmondson, "Welcome to Family History Month," *Find My Past Blog* (https://blog.findmypast.com/welcome-to-family-history-month-2026300028.html : posted 16 October 2016).

109. Ruth Randall to E.S. Mills, email, 25 August 2016.

110. Neuenschwander, "Bridges and Eternal Keepsake."

111. Stefan Walters, quoted in Rebecca Hardy, "Why Children Need to Know Their Family History," *The Guardian* (https://www.theguardian.com/lifeandstyle/2017/jan/14/children-family-histories-tales : posted 14 January 2017).

112. Maya Angelou, quoted in Joy Washington, "USA Voices in Black History, Part Two," *University of South Alabama* (http

References ⟶

://www.southalabama.edu/departments/publicrelations/pressreleases/021916blackhistoryvoices2.html : posted 19 February 2016).

113. Denis Waitley, quoted in Louise Hart, *The Winning Family: Increasing Self-Esteem in Your Children and Yourself,* rev. ed. (Berkeley, Calif.: Celestial Arts, 1996), 161.

114. E. S. Mills, posting on personal page, *Facebook* (https://www.facebook.com/elizabeth.shownmills) : posted 26 February 2015).

115. Anthony Powell, forum posting, Association of Professional Genealogists, 18 December 2011.

116. Carolyn Earle Billingsley, forum posting, Association of Professional Genealogists, 21 April 2009.

117. Chris Staats, posting on personal page, *Facebook* (https://www.facebook.com/chris.staats1?fref=ts : posted 5 September 2016).

118. E. S. Mills, "Genealogy in the Information Age: History's New Frontier?" *National Genealogical Society Quarterly* 91 (December 2003): 277.

119. Wright, "The Story Tellers."

120. Rosemary Alva, response to query by "The Genealogy Girl," 23 August 2014; appended to "Because We Don't Have an Elephant's Memory," *The Inspired Story* (https://rosemaryalva.com/2014/05/23/because-we-dont-have-an-elephants-memory/ : accessed 15 October 2016).

121. Condensed from Dan Rottenberg, *Finding Our Fathers: A Guidebook to Jewish Genealogy* (1977; reprint, Baltimore, Md.: Genealogical Publishing Co., 1977), 5.

122. Burroughs, *Black Roots,* 36.

123. Neuenschwander, "Bridges and Eternal Keepsakes."

124. Megan Smolenyak Smolenyak to Robin Roberts, con-

versation, ABC, *Good Morning America,* 2 November 2006; quoted in Smolenyak, email, 25 August 2016.

125. Carl Sandburg, *Remembrance Rock* (New York: Houghton Mifflin, 1991), 19.

126. Frequently attributed to Mark Twain, as with *The Free Dictionary by Farlex* (http://forum.thefreedictionary.com /postst3831_All-generalizations-are-false--including-this-one-.aspx : posted 1 October 2009; accessed 1 January 2017).

127. Angie Bush, "Developing a Testing Plan," 13 January 2015, Advanced Genetic Genealogy Track, Salt Lake Institute of Genealogy, Salt Lake City, Utah.

128. Debbie Parker Wayne, "Going Nuclear: DNA Discoveries to Trace All Lines of Descent," Federation of Genealogical Societies, *Journey through Generations,* annual conference syllabus (Austin, Tex: FGS, 2013), 153.

129. Eva Goodwin, "Traditional vs. Nontraditional Families," *Association of Professional Genealogists Quarterly* 29 (June 2014): 93.

130. Donn Devine, "DNA—Proof or Just Indication?" message, Transitional Genealogists Forum, 18 August 2012; archived *RootsWeb* (http://archiver.rootsweb.ancestry.com/th /read/TRANSITIONAL-GENEALOGISTS-FORUM/2012-08/1345 276256 : accessed 15 October 2016).

131. Debbie Parker Wayne, "Adding DNA Analysis to Client and Research Reports," *Association of Professional Genealogists Quarterly* 29 (June 2014): 101.

132. Bettinger, "DNA and the Genealogical Proof Standard," 435.

133. Judy G. Russell, "DNA and the Golden Rule: The Law and Ethics of Genetic Genealogy," National Genealogical Society, *Virginia: The First Frontier,* annual conference syllabus (Arlington, Va.: NGS, 2014), 477–78.

References ⟶

134. Diahan Southard, "Every Surname in Your Pedigree Can Benefit from YDNA Testing," Federation of Genealogical Societies, *Time Travel: Centuries of Memories,* annual conference syllabus (Austin, Tex.: FGS, 2016), 285.

135. Debbie Parker Wayne, "Autosomal DNA and Genealogical Research," *OnBoard* 19 (September 2013): 17.

136. Goodwin, "Traditional vs. Nontraditional Families," 93.

137. Southard, "Every Surname in Your Pedigree Can Benefit from YDNA Testing," 286.

138. E. S. Mills, *QuickSheet: Citing Genetic Sources for History Research, Evidence Style,* 2nd ed. (Baltimore: Genealogical Publishing Co., 2017), leaf 1.

139. Wayne, "Autosomal DNA and Genealogical Research," 17.

140. Donald Lines Jacobus, *Genealogy as Pastime and Profession,* rev. 2nd ed. (Baltimore: Genealogical Publishing Co., 1968), 39.

141. Peter Hoeg, *The History of Danish Dreams,* Barbara Haveland, transl. (New York: Farrar, Straus & Giroux, 1995), 152–53.

142. Elbert Hubbard, quoted by Edmund Fuller, *6200+ Wise Cracks, Witty Remarks, & Epigrams for All Occasions* (New York: Wings Books, 1993), 155.

143. Susan Sontag, quoted in Jonathan Cott, *Susan Sontag: The Complete Rolling Stone Interview* (New Haven, Conn.: Yale University Press, 2013), 34.

144. "Marcus Garvey Quotes," *Goodreads* (http://www.good reads.com/author/quotes/28955.Marcus_Garvey : accessed 2 December 2016).

145. Enrico Firmi, quoted in Tatjana Jevremovic, *Nuclear Principles in Engineering* (New York: Springer, 2005), 397.

146. Thomas E. Kida, *Don't Believe Everything You Think:*

➤ References

The 6 Basic Mistakes We Make in Thinking (Amherst, N.Y.: Promethus Books, 2006).

147. Robert Charles Anderson, "Documenting New England's Founders in the Great Migration Directory," *American Ancestors* 16 (Spring 2015): 27.

148. Mills, *QuickSheet: The Historical Biographer's Guide to the Research Process*, leaf 3.

149. Adapted from Raymond, "Frankenstein Genealogy."

150. Mills, *QuickSheet: The Historical Biographer's Guide to Cluster Research*, leaf 1.

151. Helen V. Smith, "Lost in Australia," Federation of Genealogical Societies, *Time Travel: Centuries of Memories*, annual conference syllabus (Austin, Tex.: FGS, 2016), 230.

152. Laura Murphy DeGrazia, "Should You Believe Your Eyes? Sizing Up Sources and Information," National Genealogical Society, *The Ohio River: Gateway to the Western Frontier*, annual conference syllabus (Arlington, Va.: NGS, 2012), 490.

153. Mills, "7 Ways to Jumpstart Your Research."

154. Paul Drake, message to VA-ROOTS, list-serve, 19 May 2010.

155. Fern K. Buford-Walker, message to VA-ROOTS, 19 May 2010.

156. Penelope Christensen, *How Do I Prove It?* (Toronto, Ontario: Heritage Productions, 2000), 88.

157. Terrence M. Punch, "Fishing or Researching?" *Genealogical Pointers*, e-newsletter of Genealogical Publishing Co., 27 December 2011.

158. Paul Rawlings, message, Association of Professional Genealogists list-serve, 18 September 2009.

159. Richard S. Lackey, "Genealogical Research in the

References

Lower South," seminar, Arkansas Genealogical Society, Little Rock, Ark., 14 October 1978.

160. Hait, "Why I Do Not Use Genealogy Database Software," 153.

161. Stefani Evans, "Genealogy: Targeted Biographies Give Us Layers of Knowledge," *Las Vegas Sun,* 15 July 2009; archived online, *Las Vegas Sun* (http://lasvegassun.com/news /2009/jul/15/targeted-biographies-add-layers-knowledge/ : accessed 15 October 2016).

162. Jacqueline Wilson, message, Transitional Genealogists Forum, 20 March 2010.

163. Don Anderson, "Cyberexchange 101: Learn the Tech to Trace Your Roots," luncheon presentation, 5 September 2009, Federation of Genealogical Societies annual conference, Little Rock, Ark.

164. Kim Hubbard, quoted at *Quotes* (www.quotes.net/ authors/Kim+Hubbard : accessesd 9 September 2016). A version of this ("It's what you learn after you know it all ...") also appears in John Wooden, *Wooden on Leadership: How to Create a Winning Organization* (New York: McGraw-Hill Education, 2005), 34. We have not been able to determine which quote preceded the other, but find the Hubbard version pithier.

165. Paul Milner, "Creating and Delivering a Genealogical Lecture," National Genealogical Society *NewsMagazine* 32 (October–December 2006): 39.

166. George G. Morgan, "Customizing Your Presentation Content," *Association of Professional Genealogists Quarterly* 28 (June 2013): 97.

167. Elissa Scalise Powell, forum message, Board for Certification of Genealogists ACTION group, 18 October 2016.

References

168. Dalai Lama XIV, quoted in *The Dalai Lama Book of Quotes,* Travis Hellstrom, ed. (Hobart, N.Y.: Hatherleigh Press, 2016), section "Wisdom."

169. Daniel Hubbard, "Mapping the Past: Navigating Your Family History with Maps," Federation of Genealogical Societies, *Journey through Generations,* annual conference syllabus (Austin, Tex: FGS, 2013), 249.

170. Michael G. Hait, forum posting, Association of Professional Genealogists, 13 December 2011.

171. Stefani Evans, "Oh, the Things You Can Map: Mapping Data, Memory, and Historical Context," National Genealogical Society, *Virginia: The First Frontier,* annual conference syllabus (Arlington, Va.: NGS, 2014), 184.

172. James Dannenberg, "What I Did Was Legal, But Was It Right? *Newsweek,* 18 February 2002, 19.

173. Rosie O'Donnell, "From Rosie," *Rosie* magazine (September 2001): 4.

174. Ruth Ann Abels Hager, "Tools for Discovering Missing Links: Dred and Harriet Scott, a Case Study," National Genealogical Society, *Crossroads of America,* annual conference syllabus (Arlington, Va.: NGS, 2015), 363.

175. J. H. Fonkert, "Anatomy of a Genealogy Research Report," National Genealogical Society, *Follow Your Ancestral Trail,* annual conference syllabus (Arlington, Va.: NGS, 2010), 527.

176. Isabel Wilkerson, *The Warmth of Other Sons: The Epic Story of America's Great Migration* (New York: Random House/Vintage, 2011), 538, writing of the twentieth-century African-American migration from the South to the North.

177. Robert Raymond, "Serendipity in Graveyards and Digital Scans," *The Ancestry Insider* (http://www.ancestry-

insider.org/2016/05/serendipity-in-graveyards-and-digital.
html : posted 27 May 2016).

178. Henry Z Jones Jr., *More Psychic Roots: Further Adventures in Serendipity & Intuition in Genealogy* (Baltimore: Genealogical Publishing Co., 1997), 220.

179. Mark Twain, quoted in Gerald F. Lieberman, *3,500 Good Quotes for Speakers* (Garden City, N.J.: Doubleday, 1983), 177.

180. Diedre Erin Denton, "Twisted Twigs on Gnarled Branches Genealogy," timeline post, *Facebook* (https://www.facebook.com/TwistedTwigsGenealogy/photos/a.2780711122
58211.62427.269836083081714/1200691209996192/?type=3&t
heater : 1 January 2016).

181. Randy Cantrell, "Don't Cling to a Mistake Just Because You Spent a Lot of Time Making It," *Leaning Toward Wisdom* (http://leaningtowardwisdom.com/dont-cling-to-a-mistake-just-because-you-spent-a-lot-of-time-making-it-4094/
: posted 28 July 2016).

182. Donald Lines Jacobus, as often quoted by David L. Greene, who inherited Jacobus's journal, *The American Genealogist,* and remains its consulting editor.

183. Yvette Hoitink, posting on personal page, *Facebook* (https://www.facebook.com/yvette.hoitink?ref=br_rs : posted 11 November 2016).

184. E. S. Mills, *Evidence Explained: Citing History Sources from Artifacts to Cyberspace,* 1st to 3rd eds. (Baltimore: Genealogical Publishing Co., 2007–17), §1.20.

185. David Henige, *Historical Evidence and Argument* (Madison: University of Wisconsin, 2005), 175.

186. E. S. Mills, "QuickLesson 17: The Evidence Analysis Process Map," *Evidence Explained: Historical Analysis, Citation & Source Usage* (https://www.evidenceexplained.com

/content/quicklesson-17-evidence-analysis-process-map : posted 3 August 2013).

187. Lee Albright and Helen F. M. Leary, "Designing Research Strategies," *North Carolina Research: Genealogy and Local History,* Helen F. M. Leary, ed., 2nd ed. (Raleigh: N.C. Genealogical Society, 1996), 17.

188. Stefani Evans, "Genealogy: Tricky Transcription Calls for Careful Sleuthing," *Las Vegas Sun,* 4 March 2009; archived online, *Las Vegas Sun* (http://lasvegassun.com/news/2009/mar/04/tricky-transcrition-calls-careful-sleuthing/ : accessed 15 October 2016).

189. Duncan B. Gardiner, quoted by Kathy Gunter Sullivan, message, Transitional Genealogists Forum, 10 February 2010; archived, "Transitional-GeneaLogist-Forum-L-Archives," *RootsWeb* (http://archiver.rootsweb.ancestry.com/th/read/transitional-genealogists-forum/2010-02/1265847828 : accessed 15 October 2016).

190. E. S. Mills, "Finding Fathers: Bridging the Generation Gap," Federation of Genealogical Societies, *Journey through Generations,* annual conference syllabus (Austin, Tex: FGS, 2013), 393.

191. Maureen A. Taylor, "Every Picture Tells a Story: Dating Family Photographs," National Genealogical Society, *Follow Your Ancestral Trail,* annual conference syllabus (Arlington, Va.: NGS, 2010), 561.

192. Russel E. Curran, quoted in Mark McCutcheon, *Roget's Super Thesaurus* (Cincinnati, Ohio: Writers Digest Books, 2010), 442.

193. Augustus Toplady, as quoted in William Safire and Leonard Safire, *Good Advice* (New York: Wings Books, 1982), 373.

194. Sir Robert Burton, cited in "Plagiarism Quotes, Quo-

References

tations, and Sayings," *World of Quotes.com* (www.worldof
quotes.com/topic/plagiarism/1/ : accessed 15 October 2016).

195. Claire E. White, "A Conversation with Nora Roberts,"
The Internet Writing Journal (http://www.writerswrite.com/
journal/jun98/a-conversation-with-nora-roberts-6981 : accessed 15 October 2016).

196. Smolenyak, email, 25 August 2016.

197. Rick Bragg, *All Over But the Shoutin'* (New York: Pan-
theon Books, 1997), xvi.

198. E. S. Mills, "Tracking Elusive Ancestors: There's No
Such Thing as 'Too Poor to Trace," 21 November 2015, seminar
Middle Tennessee Genealogical Society, Brentwood, Tenn.

199. Debbie Mieszala, "Twentieth and Twenty-First Cen-
tury Research: Resources, Methods, and Skills," Federation
of Genealogical Societies, *Journey through Generations,* annual conference syllabus (Austin, Tex: FGS, 2013), 276.

200. Melinde Lutz Byrne and Thomas W. Jones, "Editors'
Corner: A Grandmother's Secret," *National Genealogical Society Quarterly* 104 (June 2016): 83.

201. Rachal Mills Lennon, "The Wives of Jonathan Turner:
Identification of Women in Pre-Twentieth-Century South
Carolina," *National Genealogical Society Quarterly* 92 (De-
cember 2004): 245.

202. Mills, "Introduction to Problem Solving," various
years 1986–99, Advanced Research Methodology & Evidence
Analysis track, Samford University IGHR.

203. Lennon, "Wives of Jonathan Turner," 245.

204. E. S. Mills, *QuickSheet: Genealogical Problem Analysis—A Strategic Plan,* 1st ed. rev. (Baltimore: Genealogical
Publishing Co., 2017), leaf 1.

205. Elissa Scalise Powell, message, Transitional Genealogists Forum, 30 April 2009.

➤ References

206. Darcie M. Hind Posz, "Achieving Sustainability in the Digital Age," *Association of Professional Genealogists Quarterly* 34 [27] (March 2012): 297.

207. Steve Jobs, "'Find What You Love': Steve Jobs at Samford University," *The Wall Street Journal* (http://www.wsj.com/articles/SB10001424053111903596904576520690515394766 : updated 24 August 2011; accessed 15 October 2016).

208. Wayne, "Adding DNA Analysis to Client and Research Reports," 101.

209. Hait, "Meeting the Genealogical Proof Standard in a Client Research Project," 183.

210. Posz, "Achieving Sustainability in the Digital Age," 297.

211. Elissa Scalise Powell, personal desk motto; cited in Powell, email to Mills, 17 October 2016.

212. Harold Henderson, "Professionals and Amateurs: The Etiquette of Error, or Learning How to Disagree," *Association of Professional Genealogists Quarterly* 29 (June 2014): 97.

213. Powell, email, 17 October 2016.

214. Angie Bush, "The Genomics Revolution," *Association of Professional Genealogists Quarterly* 29 (June 2014): 85; citing "Advice on How to Research Family History," Part 2, *New York Times* (www.nytimes.com/2013/11/06/booming.advice-on-how-to-research-family-history-part-2.html : posted 13 November 2013).

215. E. S. Mills, "QuickLesson 8: What Constitutes Proof?" *Evidence Explained: Historical Analysis, Citation & Source Usage* (https://www.evidenceexplained.com/content/quicklesson-8-what-constitutes-proof : posted 28 May 2012).

216. Thomas W. Jones, "Inferential Genealogy: Deducing Ancestors' Identities Indirectly," National Genealogical Society, *The Ohio River: Gateway to the Western Frontier,* annual conference syllabus (Arlington, Va.: NGS, 2012), 79.

References

217. Helen F. M. Leary, "Psychological Frameworks for Tracking Men and Women," Advanced Research Methodology & Evidence Analysis track, 1994, Samford University IGHR.

218. Barbara Vines Little, "Ladies and Gentlemen of the Jury: The Evidence Presented Clearly Shows ... ," National Genealogical Society, *The Ohio River: Gateway to the Western Frontier*, annual conference syllabus (Arlington, Va.: NGS, 2012), 79.

219. Donn Devine, "Classifying Factors that Affect Genealogical Credibility," *OnBoard* 17 (September 2011): 23.

220. Laura Murphy DeGrazia, "What Exactly Is a 'Reasonably Exhaustive Search'?" National Genealogical Society, *Where the Past Is Still Present*, annual conference syllabus (Arlington, Va.: NGS, 2011), 230.

221. Mills, *QuickSheet: The Historical Biographer's Guide to Cluster Research*, leaf 1.

222. Mills, *QuickSheet: The Historical Biographer's Guide to the Research Process*, leaf 4.

223. Denzel Washington as "Alonzo Harris," Warner Brothers, *Training Day* (2001); quoted at "Training Day: Quotes," *IMDb* (http://www.imdb.com/title/tt0139654/quotes : accessed 15 October 2016). Appreciation to Michael Nolden Henderson, author of *Got Proof: My Genealogical Journrey Through the Use of Documentation* (Suwanee, Ga,: The Write Image, 2013), for calling this to my attention.

224. Devine, "Classifying Factors that Affect Genealogical Credibility," 23.

225. Mills, *Evidence Explained*, flyleaf, "Evidence Analysis Process Model."

226. Jones, *Mastering Genealogical Proof*, 3.

227. Ibid., 5.

228. Powell, "Beating the Bushes," 408.

229. A. C. "Tony" Proctor, posting on personal page, *Facebook* (https://www.facebook.com/ACProctor : posted 26 October 2016).

230. E. S. Mills, "What Kind of Source is *This?* Original? Derivative? Primary? Secondary? Direct? Whatchamacallit?" National Genealogical Society, *Follow Your Ancestral Trail,* annual conference syllabus (Arlington, Va.: NGS, 2010), 157.

231. Jones, "Maximizing Your Use of Evidence," 352.

232. Adapted from Barbara Vines Little, "Convincing Your Audience: How to Construct a Proof Statement," National Genealogical Society, *Where the Past Is Still Present,* annual conference syllabus (Arlington, Va.: NGS, 2011), 529.

233. Diana Crisman Smith, "Personal Style Guide," *Association of Professional Genealogists Quarterly* 33 [26] (September 2011): 149.

234. Woodtor, *Finding a Place Called Home,* 71.

235. Yvette Hoitink, "Benefits of Reasonably Exhaustive Research," *Dutch Genealogy* (https://www.dutchgenealogy.nl/benefits-of-reasonably-exhaustive-research : posted 4 November 2016).

236. E. S. Mills, "The Genealogical Proof Standard in Action," presentation, Federation of Genealogical Societies annual conference, Knoxville, Tenn., 18–21 August 2010, session F-344.

237. Jones, "Perils of Source Snobbery," 15.

238. McGhie, "What Happens When We Do Not Follow Standards?" 177.

239. David McDonald, "Top Ten Tips to Concluding Effective Research," session S-451, 14 May 2011, National Genea-

logical Society annual conference, Charleston, S.C.

240. Michael Hait, "Reasonably Exhaustive Research as a Process of Elimination," *Planting the Seeds: Genealogy as a Profession* (https://michaelhait.wordpress.com/2014/03/24/research-as-reduction : posted 24 March 2014; accessed 15 October 2016).

241. Devine, "DNA—Proof or Just Indication?"

242. Little, "Working with Documents: The Importance of Context in Record Analysis," 575.

243. Craig R. Scott, "Pension Research: You Stopped Too Soon," National Genealogical Society, *The Ohio River: Gateway to the Western Frontier,* annual conference syllabus (Arlington, Va.: NGS, 2012).

244. Sarah Larson, "The War of 1812 Papers of the State Department," *Our Family, Our Town,* Timothy Walch, ed. (Washington, D.C.: National Archives and Records Administration, 1987), 67.

245. E. S. Mills, "QuickLesson 7: FamilyLore and Indian Princesses," *Evidence Explained: Historical Analysis, Citation & Source Usage* (https://www.evidenceexplained.com/content/quicklesson-7-family-lore-and-indian-princesses : posted 22 May 2012).

246. E. S. Mills, "Smiths and Joneses: Success with Families of Common Name," Federation of Genealogical Societies, *Journey through Generations,* annual conference syllabus (Austin, Tex: FGS, 2013), 138.

247. Woodtor, *Finding a Place Called Home,* 249.

248. Elissa Scalise Powell, message, Transitional Genealogists Forum, 31 January 2010; archived "Transitional-Genealogists-Forum-L-Archives," *RootsWeb* (http://archiver.rootsweb.ancestry.com/th/read/transitional-genealogists-forum/2010-01/1264972630 : accessed 15 October 2016).

⟶ References

249. Rick Page, *Hope is Not a Strategy: The Six Keys to Winning the Complex Sale* (New York: McGraw-Hill Education, 2003).

250. E. S. Mills, "Trousers, Black Domestic, Tacks & Housekeeping Bills: 'Trivial Details' Can Solve Research Problems," Federation of Genealogical Societies, *Journey through Generations,* annual conference syllabus (Austin, Tex: FGS, 2013), 224.

251. Devine, "Classifying Factors that Affect Genealogical Credibility," 17.

252. E. S. Mills, "Genealogical Mindset and Principles of Scholarship," various years 2001–13, Advanced Research Methodology & Evidence Analysis track, Samford University IGHR.

253. E. S. Mills, "Smiths & Joneses: Success with Families of Common Names," session F-337, 2 September 2016, Federation of Genealogical Societies annual conference, Springfield, Ill.

254. Barbara Renick, "Finding Newspapers Using Online Resources," National Genealogical Society, *Where the Past Is Still Present,* annual conference syllabus (Arlington, Va.: NGS, 2011), 95.

255. Mills, "Tracking Elusive Ancestors: There's No Such Thing as 'Too Poor to Trace.'"

256. E. S. Mills, "Genealogical Problem-Solving," Advanced Research Methodology & Evidence Analysis track 4, 1986–2001, Samford University IGHR.

257. Dan Brown, *The Lost Symbol* (New York: Anchor Books/Random House, 2012), 117.

258. Mills, "Genealogical Mindset."

259. Albright and Leary, "Designing Research Strategies," 17.

References ➤

260. Jones, "Maximizing Your Use of Evidence," 352.

261. E. S. Mills, "Finding & Using Birth, Marriage & Death Records Prior to Vital Registration," National Genealogical Society, *Follow Your Ancestral Trail,* annual conference syllabus (Arlington, Va.: NGS, 2010), 495.

262. Burroughs, *Black Roots,* 20.

263. Marquetta L. Goodwine, *The Legacy of Ibo Landing: Gullah Roots of African American Culture* (Atlanta, Ga.: Clarity Press, 1998), 13.

264. Hodding S. Carter, *Where Main Street Meets the River* (New York: Rinehart, 1953), 337.

265. Woodtor, *Finding a Place Called Home,* 10.

266. Rev. C. Bernard Ruffin III, "In Search of the Unappreciated Past: The Ruffin-Cornick Family of Virginia," *National Genealogical Society Quarterly* 81 (June 1993): 126.

267. Woodtor, *Finding a Place Called Home,* 213.

268. Condensed from Hait, "Why I Do Not Use Genealogy Database Software," 153.

269. *SearchQuotes* (http://www.searchquotes.com/Technology/quotes/about/Problems : accessed 15 October 2016), commentary on the subject of problems, with quote from Stephen R. Covey, *The 7 Habits of Highly Effective People* (New York: Simon & Schuster 2013), 48.

270. Greenwood, *Researcher's Guide to American Genealogy,* 10.

271. Jones, "Perils of Source Snobbery," 9.

272. Christopher Candy, Department of History University of Durham, UK, "What, Primary Sources Again?" message, *Google Groups: sci-archaeology* (https://groups.google.com/forum/#!topic/sci.archaeology/OH3Eder1QLA%5B101-125%5D : posted 9 May 2005; accessed 28 January 2017).

➤ References

273. Jones, "Perils of Source Snobbery," 15.

274. Stefani Evans, "Check Information by Going to Original Sources," *Las Vegas Sun,* 17 June 2009; archived online, *Las Vegas Sun* (http://lasvegassun.com/news/2009/jun/17/check-information-going-original-sources/ : accessed 15 October 2016).

275. Jones, "Perils of Source Snobbery," 10.

276. Donald J. Mosemann, forum message, Board for Certification of Genealogists ACTION group, 20 April 2016.

277. Undated Facebook meme attributed to "Steve Gamlin: The Motivational Firewood Guy," *Facebook* (https://www.facebook.com/Steve.Gamlin.Author.Speaker.Motivationalist/?fref=ts : in circulation 1 September 2016).

278. Michael Ramage to E. S. Mills, email, 16 August 2016.

279. Condensed from Elissa Scalise Powell, "President's Corner," *OnBoard* 19 (May 2013): 19.

280. Mills, "What Kind of Source is This?" 157.

281. Stephen Ray Gould, *Full House: The Spread of Excellence from Plato to Darwin* (New York: Random House, Harmony Books, 1997), 57.

282. Wright, "The Story Tellers."

283. Extracted from Judy G. Russell, "The Seanachie: Linking Life and the Law through Storytelling," National Genealogical Society, *Virginia: The First Frontier,* annual conference syllabus (Arlington, Va.: NGS, 2014), 409–10.

284. Studs Terkel, quoted at *Goodreads* (https://www.goodreads.com/quotes/37584-people-are-hungry-for-stories-it-s-part-of-our-very : accessed 15 October 2016).

285. Madeleine L'Engle in "Tell Me a Story," *The Quiet Center: Women Reflecting on Life's Passages from the Pages of* Victoria Magazine (New York: Hearst Books, 1997), 163 ff.

References

286. Powell, email, 19 August 2015.

287. Mills, "Finding & Using Birth, Marriage & Death Records Prior to Vital Registration," 495.

288. Mills, *QuickSheet: Citing Genetic Sources for History Research,* leaf 1.

289. David E. Rencher, "Strategies for a Sound Beginning for Your Irish Research," Federation of Genealogical Societies, *Time Travel: Centuries of Memories,* annual conference syllabus (Austin, Tex: FGS, 2016), 172.

290. Hait, "Why I Do Not Use Genealogy Database Software," 153.

291. A. C. Ivory, *Find My Ancestor* (www.findmyancestor.com : accessed 18 August 2016), meme, undated posting.

292. Robert Heinlein, quoted at *ThinkExist* (http://thinkexist.com/quotation/when_one_teaches-two_learn/149371.html : accessed 15 October 2016).

293. Melinde Lutz Byrne to E. S. Mills, email, 19 September 2016.

294. William Lashner, *Veritas: A Novel* (New York: Regan Books, 1997), 358.

295. Donald R. Wright, "Koli Tengela in Sonko Traditions of Origin: An Example of the Process of Change in Mandinka Oral Tradition," *History in Africa* 5 (1978): 257.

296. E. S. Mills, "Oral History, Documentary Evidence, Core Truths & Genealogical Standards," National Genealogical Society, *They Passed This Way,* annual conference syllabus (Arlington, Va.: NGS, 2006), 33.

297. E. S. Mills, "Oral History's Role in Family History," presentation, American Library Association annual conference, Anaheim, Calif., June 2008.

298. James Walton, "John Walton, English Immigrant,

References

New Hampshire Native or Phantom?" *National Genealogical Society Quarterly* 102 (December 2014): 253.

299. Lennon, *Tracing Ancestors among the Five Civilized Tribes,* 16.

300. Mills, "Trousers, Black Domestic, Tacks & Housekeeping Bills," 224.

301. Woody, *RootsWeb Review,* 28 April 1999.

302. Thomas W. Jones, "Pedagogical Considerations vs. Standards—More Thoughts," email to E. S. Mills, 7 August 2012.

303. Jan Alpert, "Using and Evaluating County Histories and Published Genealogies," National Genealogical Society, *Follow Your Ancestral Trail,* annual conference syllabus (Arlington, Va.: NGS, 2010), 394.

304. Brené Brown, *The Gifts of Imperfection* (Center City, Minn.: Hazelden Publishing, 2010), 67.

305. David Clapp, posting at "Elizabeth Shown Mills," *Facebook* (https://www.facebook.com/elizabeth.showmills : posted 26 January 2012).

306. Walter Kronkite, "Both Sides of the Story," 3 October 2007 interview with Jimmy Hoffa; archived at *CBS News* (http://www.cbsnews.com/videos/both-sides-of-the-story/. : accessed 15 October 2016).

307. Attributed to Barbara Kingsolver in Russ Kick, *Quotes That Will Change Your Life* (San Francisco, Calif.: Plum Island Press, 2015), 13.

308. Robert Winks, *The Historian as Detective: Essays on Evidence* (New York: Harper Colophon Books, 1968), 39.

309. Robert Raymond, "Darned Image Citations," *The Ancestry Insider* (http://www.ancestryinsider.org/2016/08/darned-image-citations.html : posted 5 August 2016).

References

310. "Alduous Huxley on Truth and Madness," quoted at David Pearce, *Aldous Huxley* (https://www.huxley.net/ah/ah prof.html : accessed 15 October 2016).

311. Flannery O'Connor, *The Habit of Being: Letters of Flannery O'Connor,* Sally Fitzgerald, ed. (1979; reprint, New York: Farrar, Straus & Giroux, 1998), 100.

312. Byrne and Jones, "Editors' Corner: A Grandmother's Secret," 83.

313. Wayne, "Adding DNA Analysis to Client and Research Reports," 101.

314. Greenwood, *Researcher's Guide to American Genealogy,* 12.

315. Richard Feynman, *The Pleasure of Finding Things Out: The Best Short Works of Richard Feynman,* Jeffrey Robbins, ed. (New York: Basic Books, 1999), 24.

316. Stefani Evans, "Genealogy: Gas Receipts Help Track 1966 Road Trip," *Las Vegas Sun,* 1 December 2008; archived at *Las Vegas Sun* (http://lasvegassun.com/news/2008/dec/11 /gas-receipts-help-track-1933-road-trip/ : accessed 15 October 2016).

317. Hendrix, "Going Beyond the Database," 133.

318. E. S. Mills, "Using Tax Rolls to Prove Births, Deaths, Marriages, Parentage & Origin," session S-408, 3 September 2016, Federation of Genealogical Societies annual conference, Springfield, Ill.

319. Max Anders, *30 Days to Understanding the Bible* (Nashville, Tenn.: Thomas Nelson, 2011), 22.

320. Little, "Working with Documents," 575.

321. E. S. Mills, "Hell on the Homefront! War-Time Damages & the Claims They Generated," National Genealogical Society, *Follow Your Ancestral Trail,* annual conference syllabus (Arlington, Va.: NGS, 2010), 333.

➤ References

322. Scott, "Pension Research: You Stopped Too Soon," 213.

323. Donn Devine, e-mail message, Transitional Genealogists Forum, 29 January 2010; archived in "Transitional-Genealogists-Forum-L-Archives," *RootsWeb* (http://archiver.roots web.ancestry.com/th/read/transitional-genealogists-forum /2010-01/1264750937 : accessed 15 October 2016).

324. "Valerie Eichler Lair," personal page, *Facebook* (https ://www.facebook.com/valerie.e.lair : posted 13 September 2015), comment by E.S. Mills.

325. Quoted in George Plimpton and Frank H. Crowther, "E. B. White, The Art of the Essay No. 1," *The Paris Review* (Fall 1969), page numbers not cited; archived online, *The Paris Review* (http://www.theparisreview.org/interviews/4155/the -art-of-the-essay-no-1-e-b-white : accessed 15 October 2016).

326. Flannery O'Connor, quoted in J. M. Bohannon, *I Hate Writing: The Unofficial Guide to Freshman Composition and Undergraduate Writing* (New York: iUniverse, 2005), 11.

327. Stefani Evans, "Editing Makes a Difference," *Las Vegas Sun,* 3 September 2009; archived, *Las Vegas Sun* (http://las vegassun.com/news/2009/sep/02/editing-makes-differ- ence/ : accessed 15 October 2016).

328. John Philip Colletta," Writing a Family History: Snares and Pitfalls," National Genealogical Society, *Virginia: The First Frontier,* annual conference syllabus (Arlington, Va.: NGS, 2014), 467.

329. Linda Coffin, "Writing for Your Audience: Who Will Read Your Family History?" in National Genealogical Society, *Virginia: The First Frontier,* annual conference syllabus (Arlington, Va.: NGS, 2014), 391.

330. Diana Crisman Smith, "Does It Sound Like You?" *Association of Professional Genealogists Quarterly* 29 (June 2014): 99.

References

331. E. S. Mills, "Skillbuilding: Good Genealogical Writing," *OnBoard* 4 (May 1998): 16.

332. Clay Mills, "6 Keys to Writing Compelling Songs," *SongTown* (https://Songtown.com/6-keys-to-writing-compelling-creative-songs/ : posted 28 August 2016).

Individuals Quoted

A

Albright, Lee. 73, 84, 97
Alpert, Jan. 114
Alva, Rosemary. 46
Anders, Max. 118
Anderson, Don. 61
Anderson, Robert Charles. 30, 56
Angelou, Maya. 44
Aniston, Jennifer. 16

B

Bach, Richard. 16
Baxter, Carol. 22
Bernard, Claude. 25
Bettinger, Blaine T. 36, 42, 50
Billingsley, Carolyn Earle. 45
Board for Certification of Genealogists. 43
Booth, Wayne C. 18
Bragg, Rick. 77
Brandt, Anthony. 38
Brown, Brené. 114
Brown, Dan. 96
Buckley, Gail Lumet. 38
Buford-Walker, Fern K. 59
Bulwer-Lytton, Edward George Earle. 36
Burroughs, Tony. 15, 32, 33, 47, 98
Burton, Robert, Sir. 76

Individuals Quoted ➤

Bush, Angie. 49
Byrne, Melinde Lutz. 78, 110, 116

C

Candy, Christopher. 103
Cantrell, Randy. 70
Carter, Debra Newman. 12
Carter, Hodding S. 99
Cellini, Benvenuto. 14
Christensen, Penelope. 59
Clapp, David. 115
Clemens, Samuel (aka Mark Twain). 48
Coffin, Linda. 121
Colletta, John Philip. 121
Covey, Stephen R. 102
Crane, Frasier (Kelsey Grammer). 39
Curran, Robert. 76

D

Dalai Lama 14th (Tenzin Gyatso). 63
Dannenberg, James. 65
DeGrazia, Laura Murphy. 58, 85
Delphin, Terrel A. 33
Denton, Diedre Erin. 69
Devine, Donn. 49, 85, 86, 91, 94, 120
Dickens, Charles. 38
Drake, Paul. 59

E

Evans, Stefani. 61, 64, 73, 104, 118, 120

Individuals Quoted

F

Fermi, Enrico. 55
Feynman, Richard. 117
Fonkert, J. H. "Jay." 66
Fontenot, Tracy Colson. 126
Freilich, Kay Haviland. 40
Fuller, Thomas. 14

G

Gamlin, Steve. 105
Gardiner, Duncan B. 73
Garvey, Marcus. 54
Goodwin, Eva. 49, 51
Goodwine, Marquetta L. 99
Gould, Stephen Jay. 12, 106
Graham, Paul K. 24
Grammer, Kelsey ("Frasier Crane"). 39
Greenwood, Val D. 11, 15, 103, 116
Gyatso, Tenzin, 14th Dalai Lama. 63

H

Hager, Ruth Ann Abels. 66
Hait, Michael G. 42, 60, 64, 82, 91, 101, 109
Hare, Alison. 21, 23
Harris, Alonzo (Denzel Washington). 86
Hartley, L. P. 18
Hatch, Orrin. 43
Heinlein, Robert. 110
Henderson, Harold. 18, 41, 82
Hendrix, GeLee Corley. 12, 118
Henige, David. 72

Individuals Quoted

Hoeg, Peter. 54
Hoitink, Yvette. 71, 90
Holmes, Oliver Wendell, I. 15
Howard, Jane. 38, 43
Hubbard, Daniel. 64
Hubbard, Elbert. 54
Hubbard, Kim. 61
Huxley, Alduous. 116

I

Ivory, A. C. 110

J

Jacobus, Donald Lines. 52, 70
Jobs, Steve. 81
Jones, Henry Z, Jr. 69
Jones, Thomas W. 11, 21, 22. 27, 35, 36, 41, 42, 78, 84, 86, 87, 90, 97, 103, 104, 114, 116
Joslyn, Roger D. 30

K

Keller, Helen. 15
Kida, Thomas E. 55
Kingsolver, Barbara. 115
Kronkite, Walter. 115

L

Lackey, Richard S. 60
Lacopo, Michael D. 16
Lacour, Lair. 126.
Larsen, Sarah. 93
Lashner, William. 111

Individuals Quoted

Leary, Helen F. M. 73, 84, 97
L'Engle, Madeleine. 107
Lennon, Rachal Mills. 34, 40, 79, 80, 112
Lincoln, Abraham. 14
Little, Barbara Vines. 23, 84, 88, 92, 118

M

Magritte, René. 26
McDonald, David. 23, 91
McDonald, Edgar. 17
McGhie, Angela Packer. 17, 91
Metoyer, Louis. 13
Mieszala, Debbie. 78
Milner, Paul. 62
Mills, Clay. 121
Mills, Elizabeth Shown. 16, 17, 19, 22, 23, 28, 29, 35, 39, 40, 45, 46, 51, 56, 58, 71, 72, 74, 77, 79, 80, 83, 84, 85, 86, 87, 90, 93, 94, 95, 96, 98, 105, 108, 111, 112, 118, 119, 120, 121
Mokotoff, Gary. 34.
Molière, Jean Baptiste Poquelin, alias. 13, 39
Morgan, George G.. 62
Moseman, Donald J. 105
Mooneeram, Roshni. 13

N

Neill, Michael John. 30
Nelson, Russel M. 14
Nightingale, Florence. 17
Nin, Anaïs. 36
Neuenschwander, Dennis B. 13, 43, 47

O

O'Connor, Flannery. 116, 120

Individuals Quoted

O'Donnell, Rosie. 65
Overmire, Laurence. See copyright page, dedication page.

P
Plutarch. 13
Pollard, John Garland. 43
Posz, Darcie M. Hind. 81, 82
Powell, Anthony. 45
Powell, Elissa Scalise. 22, 28, 41, 63, 81, 82, 83, 87, 94, 105, 108
Proctor, A. C. "Tony." 87
Punch, Terrence M. 59

R
Ramage, Michael. 105
Randall, Ruth. 43
Rawlings, Paul. 59
Raymond, Robert. 36, 56, 68, 115
Rencher, David E. 109
Renick, Barbara. 95
Richey, Nancy. 33
Roberts, Nora. 76
Robinson, Marilynne. 37
Rogers, Will. 11
Rottenberg, Dan. 47
Ruffin, C. Bernard III. 100
Russell, Judy G. 31, 50, 106

S
Sandburg, Carl. 47
Sayer, Pamela K. 28
Schiff, Lewis. 37
Scott, Craig Roberts. 92, 119
Smith, Diana Crisman. 88, 121

⟞Individuals Quoted

Smith, Helen V. 57
Smolenyak, Megan Smolenyak. 15, 39, 47, 77
Sontag, Susan. 54
Southard, Diahan. 50, 51
Staats, Chris. 46
Stuart-Warren, Paula. 32, 34

T

Taylor, Maureen A. 75
Terkel, Studs. 107
Thoreau, Henry David. 35
Toplady, Augustus. 76
Tufte, Edward. 35
Twain, Mark (Samuel Clemens). 48

W

Waitley, Dennis. 44
Wallace, David Foster. 20
Walters, Stefan. 44
Walton, James. 111
Washington, Denzel ("Alonzo Harris"). 86
Wayne, Debbie Parker. 49, 50, 51, 81, 116
White, E. B. 120
Whitehead, Alfred North. 12
Wilde, Oscar. 15
Wilkerson, Isabel. 67
Wilson, Jacqueline. 61
Winks, Robert. 115
Woodtor, Dee Parmer. 11, 12, 19, 32, 33, 89, 93, 100
Woody, David. 27, 114
Wright, Della M. Cummings. 37, 46, 106
Wright, Donald R. 111

Keywords

A

Abilities. *See* Trivial Details.

Abstract. *See* Negative Findings.

Accidents. *See* Families *and* Standards.

Accreditation. *See* Credentials.

Accuracy. *See that category. Also* Errors, Questions, *and* Sources.

African Americans. *See* Ethnic Research, Genealogy, *and* Silence.

American folk sayings. *See* Migration, Sources, *and* Trust.

Analysis. *See that category. Also* Caution, Document Analysis, Genealogy, *and* Research.

Ancestor hunters. *See* Accuracy.

Ancestors & Ancestry. *See that category. Also* Genealogy, Learning, Miscellany, Professional Genealogy, Research, Success, Trust, *and* Writing.

Ancestral shame. *See* Truth.

Anomalies. *See* Truth.

Associates. *See* FAN Principle, Poor Folks, *and* Research.

Assumptions. *See* Context *and* Understanding.

Audiences. *See* Lecturing.

B

Bibliographic entries. *See* Citations.

Biography. *See* Genealogy.

Biology. *See* Genetic Genealogy.

Blank spaces. *See* Land *and* Writing.

Brick walls. *See that category. Also* Reasonably Exhaustive Research.

Burned counties. *See* Elusive Ancestors *and* Origins.

~Keywords

C

Caution. *See that category. Also* Research Traps.

Censuses. *See* Maps & Mapping.

Certainties. *See* Proof.

Certification. *See* Credentials.

Chains and links. *See* Genealogy *and* Research.

Challenges. *See* Genealogy.

Charlemagne. *See* Research.

Chinese proverbs. *See* Ancestors & Ancestry.

Chosen ones. *See* Genealogy.

Citations. *See that category. Also* Documentation *and* Proof.

Civilization. *See* Genealogy.

Claims. *See* Proof.

Clans. *See* Families.

Clients. *See* Credentials, Genealogical Proof Standard, Professional Genealogy, *and* Success.

Clones. *See* Standards.

Clues. *See* Elusive Ancestors, History, Methodology, *and* Origins.

Coincidences. *See* Miscellany.

Collective memory. *See* Ethnic Research *and* Silence.

Collectors. *See* Genealogy *and* Research.

Completeness. *See* Conclusions.

Computers. *See* Internet.

Conceit. *See* Ancestors & Ancestry.

Conclusions. *See that category. Also* Citations, Genealogical Proof Standard, Methodology, Negative Evidence, Proof, Research, *and* Software.

Confidence. *See* Conclusions *and* Genealogical Proof Standard.

Conflict resolution. *See* Proof.

Conflicting evidence. *See* Genetic Genealogy *and* Proof.

Confusions. *See* Evidence.

Connections. *See* Problem Solving *and* Trivial Details.

Keywords⟶

Consistency. *See* Quality.

Context. *See that category. Also* Conclusions, Genealogy, Negative Evidence, Reasonably Exhaustive Research, Stories & Storyteling, *and* Writing.

Contradictory evidence. *See* Evidence, Proof.

Correlation. *See* Accuracy, Proof, *and* Sources.

Corroboration of facts. *See* Proof.

Creativity. *See that category. Also* Success.

Credentials. *See that category.*

Credibility. *See* Citations, Conclusions, Genealogical Proof Standard, *and* Proof.

Creoles. *See* Ethnic Research.

Crowd-sourcing. *See* Family Trees.

Cultural heritage. *See* Ethnic Research *and* Professional Genealogy.

D

Data. *See* Caution *and* Information.

Databases. *See* Analysis, Research, *and* Understanding.

Dead ends. *See* Brick Walls *and* Problem Solving.

Denial. *See* Silence.

Direct evidence. *See* Proof.

Discipline. *See* Genealogy *and* Writing.

Discovery. *See that category. Also* Hypotheses.

DNA. *See* Ethics, Evidence, Genealogical Proof Standard, Genealogy, Professional Genealogy, Reasonably Exhaustive Research, Success, *and* Truth.

Document Analysis. *See that category. Also* Analysis.

Documentation. *See that category. Also* Conclusions, Genetic Genealogy, *and* Professional Genealogy.

Documents. *See* Analysis, Document Analysis, *and* Reasonably Exhaustive Research.

E

Editing. *See that category. Also* Writing.

Education. *See that category. Also* Stories & Storytelling.

Elusive ancestors. *See that category. Also* Poor Folks.

Embarrassment. *See* Ancestors & Ancestry, Silence, *and* Truth.

Emotions. *See* Genealogy.

Errors. *See that category. Also* Accuracy, Analysis, Mistakes, Sources, *and* Uncertainty.

Ethics. *See that category.*

Ethnic research. *See that category.*

Evidence. *See that category. Also* Accuracy, Analysis, Citations, Conclusions, Creativity, Genealogical Proof Standard, Genealogy, Proof, Proof Statements, Reasonably Exhaustive Research, Research, *and* (The) Research Question.

Experience. *See* Teaching.

Explanations. *See* Facts.

F

Faces. *See* Families.

Facts. *See that category. Also* Genealogy, Information, Memoirs & Diaries, Proof, Research, *and* Writing.

Fakelore. *See* Traditions.

False assumptions. *See* Conclusions.

False information. *See* Generalizations.

Families. *See that category.*

Families, non-traditional. *See* Genetic Genealogy.

Family historians. *See* Miscellany, Reasonably Exhaustive Research, *and* Sources.

Family history. *See* Genealogy, Learning, *and* Traditions

Family narratives. *See* Writing.

Family tapestries. *See* Genealogy.

Family trees. *See that category. Also* Ancestors & Ancestry, Research, Standards, *and* Teaching.

Family wounds. *See* Genealogy.

Keywords ➤

FAN Principle. *See that category. Also* Poor Folks, Research, *and* Tax Records.

Fiction. *See* Family Trees.

Folklore. *See* Traditions.

Fools, knaves, or beggars. *See* Ancestors & Ancestry.

Footnotes, endnotes, reference notes. *See* Citations.

"Former Ancestors." *See* Reasonably Exhaustive Research.

G

Genealogical Proof Standard. *See that category. Also* Conclusions, Evidence, Genealogy, Proof, *and* Software.

Genealogists Anonymous. *See* Miscellany.

Genealogy. *See that category.*

Genealogy as a journey. *See* Miscellany.

Genealogy software. *See* Genealogical Proof Standard.

Generalizations. *See that category.*

Genes. *See* Genetic Genealogy.

Genetic Genealogy. *See that category.*

Genetic Genealogists. *See* Professional Genealogy.

Genius. *See* Problem Solving.

Geography. *See* Understanding.

Glory. *See* Ancestors & Ancestry.

Good intentions. *See* Sources.

Google. *See* Internet *and* Research.

Gospel According to Grandma. *See* Traditions.

GPS (Genealogical Proof Standard). *See that category.*

GPS (Global Positioning System). *See* Genetic Genealogy.

Grab-and-go genealogy. *See* Research.

Grandparents. *See* Miscellany.

Gullibility. *See that category. Also* Trust.

H

Handicaps. *See* Brick Walls.

Heredity. *See* Ancestors & Ancestry.

→Keywords

Heritage. *See* Ethnic Research *and* Teaching.
Historians. *See* Genealogy *and* Negative Evidence.
History. *See that category. Also* dedication page, Caution, *and* Proof.
Hope. *See* Analysis *and* Research.
House histories. *See* Maps & Mapping.
Hypotheses. *See that category. Also* Methodology *and* Proof.

I

Identity. *See that category. Also* FAN Principle, Genealogical Proof Standard, Murphy's Law, *and* Names.
Immigration. *See that category. Also* Migration.
Implications. *See* Negative Evidence.
Indexes. *See* Problem Solving *and* Research.
Indians. *See* Native Americans.
Informants. *See* Information.
Information. *See that category. Also* Genealogical Proof Standard, Proof, Software, Sources, *and* Understanding.
Inspiration. *See* Ethnic Research *and* Genealogy.
Intentions. *See* Sources.
Internet. *See that category. Also* Research.
Intuition. *See* Miscellany.
Investigations. *See* Problem Solving.

J

Jurisdictions. *See* Maps & Mapping.

K

Kinship. *See* FAN Principle, Genealogy, *and* Professional Genealogy.
Knowledge. *See* Ancestors & Ancestry, Information, *and* Professional Genealogy.

Keywords —

L

Land. *See that category. Also* Analysis, Evidence, *and* Maps & Mapping.

Laws. *See* Professional Genealogy.

Learning. *See that category.*

Lecturing. *See that category.*

Legal language. *See* Professional Genealogy.

Lies. *See* Genealogy.

Life. *See* Miscellany.

Links between facts. *See* History, Land, *and* Tax Records.

Links in a chain. See Genealogy *and* Research.

Lookups. *See* Problem Solving.

Luck. *See that category. Also* Miscellany.

M

Maps & Mapping. *See that category.*

Memoirs & Diaries. *See that category.*

Memories. *See* Ethnic Research, Genetic Genealogy, and Truth.

Methodology. *See that category. Also* Brick Walls *and* Research.

Migration. *See that category. Also* Immigration.

Miracles. *See* Miscellany.

Mirrors. *See* Families.

Miscellany. *See that category.*

Mistakes. *See that category. Also* Errors *and* Genealogy.

Money. *See* Traditions.

Murphy's Law. *See that category.*

Myths. *See* Documentation *and* Traditions.

N

Names. *See that category. Also* Proof *and* Research

Native Americans. *See* Ethnic Research *and* Traditions.

Negative Evidence. *See that category.*

Negative Findings. *See that category.*
Negative results. *See* Negative Findings.
Neighbors. *See* FAN Principle, Poor Folks, Research, *and* Tax Records.
Newspapers. *See* Research.
Nontraditional families. *See* Genetic Genealogy.
Novice genealogists. *See* Brick Walls.

O

Objectives. *See* (The) Research Question *and* Writing.
Omissions. *See* Errors.
Opportunity. *See* Luck *and* Trivial Details.
Origins. *See that category. Also* Elusive Ancestors, FAN Principle, Poor Folks, *and* Research.

P

Paper trails. *See* Genetic Genealogy, Problem Solving, Records, *and* Wars.
Past. *See* Caution, Ethnic Research *and* Silence.
Past, forgotten. *See* Genealogy.
Patterns. *See* Citations *and* Research.
Peerage. *See* Ancestors & Ancestry.
Personal histories. *See* Memoirs & Diaries.
Perspectives. *See* Professional Genealogy.
Photographs. *See that category.*
Plagiarism. *See that category.*
Plain folk. *See* Poor Folks *and* Problem Solving.
Points of view. *See* Truth.
Poor Folks. *See that category. Also* Research.
Poor recordkeeping. *See* Problem Solving.
Possibilities. *See* Brick Wall, Conclusions, *and* Evidence
Prejudice. *See* Genealogy.
Premature conclusions. *See* Conclusions, Genealogical Proof Standard, *and* Reasonably Exhaustive Research.
Preparation. *See* Lecturing, Luck, *and* Research.

Keywords⟶

Primary sources. *See* Sources.

Privacy. *See that category.*

Problem Solving. *See that category. Also* Credentials, Solutions, *and* Trivial Details.

Professional Genealogists. *See that category. Also* Success.

Proof. *See that category. Also* Conclusions, Genealogical Proof Standard, *and* Proof Statements.

Proof Statements. *See that category.*

Purpose of genealogy. *See* Ancestors & Ancestry, *and* Genealogy.

Q

Quality. *See that category.*

Questions. *See that category. Also* Accuracy *and* (The) Research Question.

R

Reasonably Exhaustive Research. *See that category. Also* Genealogy, Genealogical Proof Standard, *and* Genetic Genealogy.

Reasoning. *See* Conclusions, Evidence, *and* Identity.

Record destruction. *See* Burned Courthouses *and* Problem Solving.

Records. *See that category. Also* Creativity, Errors, *and* Tax Records.

Records, illegible. *See* Murphy's Law.

Reference notes. *See* Citations *and* Documentation.

Relationships. *See* FAN Principle, Genealogical Proof Standard, *and* Genealogy.

Reporting. *See* Research.

Research. *See that category. Also* Analysis, Brick Walls, Creativity, Genealogical Proof Standard, Methodology, Sources, *and* Teaching.

Research plans. *See* Research *and* (The) Research Question.

(The) Research Question. *See that category. Also* Evidence, Proof, *and* Reasonably Exhaustive Research.

Research Traps. *See that category. Also* Caution.

Residence. *See* Origins.

Roots. *See that category. Also* History.

Roots and wings. *See* Genealogy *and* Roots.

S

Scientific method. *See* Methodology.

Secondary sources. *See* Sources.

Secrets. *See* Ethnic Research: African American *and* Genetic Genealogy.

Self-delusion. *See* Hypotheses *and* Research.

Selfies. *See* Genealogy.

Serendipity. *See* Miscellany.

Shame. *See* Ethnic Research (African American), Silence, *and* Truth.

Shortcuts. *See* Problem Solving.

Silence. *See* Ethnic Research *and* Negative Evidence.

Situations. *See* Negative Evidence.

Skills. *See* Evidence *and* Professional Genealogy.

Slave research. *See* Ancestors & Ancestry *and* Ethnic Research.

Snapshots. *See* Censuses *and* Photographs.

Social genealogy. *See* Genealogy.

Society. *See* Genealogy.

Software. *See that category. Also* Genealogical Proof Standard.

Sound research. *See* Genealogy Proof Standard *and* Standards.

Source types. *See* Accuracy *and* Sources.

Sources. *See that category. Also* Documentation, Proof, Reasonably Exhaustive Research, *and* Standards.

Keywords —

Southern genealogy. *See* Problem Solving.
Spaces between records. *See* Land *and* Tax Records.
Spanish proverbs. *See* Ancestors & Ancestry.
Spiritual beliefs. *See* Genetic Genealogy.
Standards. *See that category. Also* Genealogical Proof Standard *and* Research.
Stepping stones. *See* Miscellany.
Stories & Storytelling. *See* Facts, Genealogy, Genetic Genealogy, Photographs, Silence, *and* Traditions.
Strategies. *See* Methodology *and* Research.
Stumbling blocks. *See* Miscellany.
Success. *See that category. Also* Ethnic Research, Genetic Genealogy, *and* Research.
Sum of the evidence. *See* Proof.
Sum of the facts. *See* Tax Records.
Supply and demand. *See* Professional Genealogy.

T

Tax Records. *See that category. Also* Analysis *and* Evidence.
Teaching. *See that category.*
Theses. *See* Hypotheses *and* Proof.
Thinking. *See* Family Trees.
Thoroughness. *See* Brick Walls, Ethnic Research, Genealogical Proof Standard, Negative Evidence, Problem Solving, *and* Reasonably Exhaustive Research.
Time-savers. *See* Writing.
Tools. *See* Genetic Genealogy *and* Success.
Traditions. *See that category. Also* Genetic Genealogy, Silence, *and* Stories & Storytelling.
Tribes. *See* Families *and* Genealogy.
Trivial details. *See that category.*
Trolling the Internet. *See* Internet *and* Research.
Trust. *See that category. Also* Documentation, Gullibility, Reasonably Exhaustive Research, *and* Sources.
Truth. *See that category. Also* Censuses, Genealogy, Memoirs & Diaries, *and* Privacy.

⟶ Keywords

U

Uncertainty. *See that category.*

Understanding. *See that category. Also* Conclusions, Professional Genealogy, *and* Writing.

V

Vacuums, genealogical. See FAN Principle *and* Genetic Genealogy.

Viewpoints. *See* Professional Genealogy *and* Truth.

W

Wars. *See that category.*

Writing. *See that category. Also* Editing.